Stanley Gene
Daydream Believer

With Stuart Wilkin

2nd edition first published in the United Kingdom by TH Media in Derbyshire in 2011

ISBN Number 978-0-9559534-0-8

Design by Strawberry

Printed in Great Britain by PrintFlow Limited, Citybridge House, 235/245 Goswell Road, London

Pictures reproduced with kind permission given by the following:
TFB Photography
Hull Daily Mail
Hull Kingston Rovers
Bradford Bulls
Huddersfield Giants

Contents

Foreword by Tony Smith

Daydream Believer

If you can dream – and not make dreams your master;
If you can think – and not make thoughts your aim;
If you can meet with Triumph and Disaster
And treat those two impostors just the same;
If you can bear to hear the truth you've spoken
Twisted by knaves to make a trap for fools,
Or watch the things you gave your life to, broken,
And stoop and build 'em up with worn-out tools:

If you can make one heap of all your winnings
And risk it on one turn of pitch-and-toss,
And lose, and start at your beginnings
And never breathe a word about your loss;
If you can force your heart and nerve and sinew
To serve your turn long after they are gone,
And so hold on when there is nothing in you
Except the Will which says to them: 'Hold on!'

If you can talk with crowds and keep your virtue,
Or walk with Kings - nor lose the common touch,
If neither foes nor loving friends can hurt you,
If all men count with you, but none too much;
If you can fill the unforgiving minute
With sixty seconds' worth of distance run,
Yours is the Earth and everything that's in it,
And – which is more – you'll be a Man my son!

Rudyard Kipling

1865-1936

Oh I could hide 'neath the wings
Of the robin as she sings.
The memories I have will never die.
And I know I'm gonna cry
Wipe a tear out of my eye.
Hull KR means everything to me.

We've been through thick and thin
But we always tried to win
Craven Park has given me so much
As the sun fades to grey
And my boots are packed away
I will stand and sing my favourite song

Cheer up Stanley Gene
Oh what can it mean?
To a Rovers supporter
And a great rugby team.

(Repeat)

Mike Smith

Happily still with us.

To Maul and Christina,

Paul and Stephanie,

Their wonderful daughter Jo

And our two boys Elliott and Leo

Daydream Believer

Foreword

Does anyone actually know how old Stanley is? People have been speculating about his age for a few years now, and I have to say that even when I signed him for Huddersfield Giants in 2001 it seemed like he'd already been around forever.

But sometimes perception isn't quite reality. For sure, he's had a long and exciting career, but maybe not quite as long as we think. You see, Stanley is one of those players who sticks in supporters' memories, by the way he plays, and he's always surprising people. Sometimes he has exceeded people's expectations, but not mine. It's only when you get to coach Stanley that you can understand why he has been successful for so long.

Neither of us were having things all our own way when we first got together. I brought Stanley from Hull at a time when things weren't going as he wanted, and we were having a tough time at Huddersfield. I knew he could contribute a whole lot to our team, but at the time I didn't realise just how much. As I got to know Stanley, it became clear to me that he is much more than a dynamic player on the field; he also has a dynamic personality and a great character. And signing him at that time gave the Giants a massive boost.

Stanley was far more of an intelligent player than I had given him credit for, and many others gave him credit for. We soon developed a relationship where I could see quite clearly how he was becoming a thinking player more than simply a dynamic player. Everyone sees how explosive he can be, particularly when he's carrying the ball but he's a very intelligent player who can read the play better than most. He brought a whole lot more, and took a far greater role within the team than I had expected.

And he just keeps going on and on. Stanley is an incredible athlete with a remarkable level of fitness. I remember at times he had injuries and I was always amazed how quickly he overcame them to get back on the field. Some people are quick healers, and Stanley certainly is, it's partly to do with his physical make-up. But he's aware of his ability to get back to fitness quicker than other athletes and he works very hard to maintain that.

To be fair, he didn't always have a great reputation for hard training. But he adapted and buckled down, and he always trained very well for me. That's maybe because I didn't ask him to swim! We often joked about him not wanting to train, but when it came down to it, he always did. And he's never been too stubborn to learn or to change. Coaches love to work with players who can change with the times. And there is no one better qualified to cope with change than Stanley. When you think of the way he adapted to life in the UK, leaving his family and home on the other side of the world, it's nothing short of awesome.

Stanley's whole approach to life keeps him young. He's a popular guy who enjoys everything he does, and he's a real pleasure to be around. I think this is partly what gives him this longevity. I'm hoping to have the pleasure of watching Stanley for a bit longer yet. The way he's playing at the moment, he's as young as ever.

And there's so much more to Stanley than just being a good rugby league player, as you'll find out. He's a person that I have a lot of admiration for. I think that's a plaudit that can sometimes be handed out too freely, but I am very sincere in saying that I really, really admire the guy. And I have the privilege to count myself as his friend.

He's been a great pleasure to coach and a terrific ambassador for the game, always happy to do his bit off the field. And he's well liked by everyone he meets. You can't fail to love the guy's warmth and humility, and he'll always make you laugh, whether he wants to or not.

The dynamism, intelligence and loyalty that have been the hallmarks of Stanley's qualities on the field of play, are characteristics that you will recognise when you read about his life. The little man is a giant Rover in many ways, and his achievements are astounding.

I'm really pleased and honoured to introduce this incredible account of his life.

Tony Smith
GB Coach

Daydream Believer

1

Back Home

2007
Hull Kingston Rovers

England is a great country to live in.

It has everything you'd ever want. There are some places of natural beauty here, and some that are really spectacular. We have lovely countryside, mountains to climb and lakes and rivers to fish in.

We also have Sky TV, the National Health Service, Morecambe and Wise and twenty-four hour Tesco's. And some of the railway stations are like shopping arcades. We have politicians that try to be taken seriously but then you see them on the telly shouting 'NAAAY' and waving bits of paper around. But actually, when they do speak proper English it's total bollocks anyway. It has a lot to do with history, and there's lots of that in England. In fact, the Queen lives here.

But at least the politicians just seem to disagree, nick each other's ideas and insult each other ... and unlike in other parts of the world they never end up dead, which is usually helpful.

The food is brilliant and there's so much of it. You can go into a Chinese takeaway, tell them your favourite numbers and come away with a feast. In Sainsbury's you can buy everything that Jamie Oliver puts in his dinner. I hadn't been here long when he came on telly on a programme called the 'Naked Chef'. I thought it was one of those 'special' shows you see on Channel 5 but he just cooked stuff with all his clothes on. Even when his sisters' friends all turned up at midnight he was still there making bacon sandwiches. I know what he was after but it never happened!

There are local delicacies wherever you go. You get fantastic fish and chips in Whitby. And in Oldham you can get something that they call a pasty barm. It's a big bread roll with a meat and potato pie in it and apparently everyone in Lancashire eats it. When I first came to Craven Park we had someone who came to the club called a nutritionist. He would turn up at the ground after training and speak to us about food. I thought it was a really strange thing to do because we all knew about food and we were paid to play rugby. But maybe I missed the point. My English wasn't at all good, but now I think about it I'm sure he was talking about the pasty barm.

♦

Everyone in England's completely sport mad and there's lots to choose from. There are loads of sports I'd never seen in my home town of Goroka, like ice hockey and synchronised swimming. The national sport of Papua New Guinea is Rugby League, and in any case, Goroka is high in the mountains and a four day drive to the coast. And we certainly didn't get much ice!

The locals in England are warm, weird, friendly and sometimes very funny. Not much different from the people of my home country. Language is a strange thing too. In Papua New Guinea we have eight hundred local dialects ....all different. But it seems to me that there are just as many languages in England. And like I say, over here people call food by different names from city to city. During my first week in Hull back in 1996, I went into a chippy on Holderness Road, and I came out with something called a patty. It was brilliant and I've eaten about three thousand since, but I still don't know exactly what it is. I'm sure it's got potato and herbs in it, and it's battered. This was really good, and it was my first week in England so I naturally assumed it was the national dish.

So when I was in Doncaster the following week, I went into a chippy and asked for patty with chips. I might as well have been back in PNG. The girl looked at me as if I'd asked for a lawnmower.

But it gets worse. If you go further across to Lancashire, in a bakery you'll see that the really small meat pies are called patties. And I later found out that throughout the whole country, if you're out for a meal you can get a starter called pate (pronounced patty).

It's all very confusing, but after twelve years I think I'm getting the hang of it.

But I do love this country. Apart from the crap weather and London. I'm not surprised the Queen spends all her time travelling the world, because in London no one knows anyone else, but they all kiss each other all the time. And at seven in the morning they all charge manically to work (everything goes so fast in London) and then at seven in the evening they all sprint to the pub.

Outside London I can see similarities between the people of Papua New Guinea and many folk I have met here. In Goroka, I learnt that whatever temptations I had and whatever fears I faced, there were qualities that I must always work hard to achieve, and always respect in others. Conviction of spirit, loyalty and honesty define a man of honour. And I have met plenty of guys in my time in England that have all those qualities. So I have always tried to live up to these standards.

In our sport, loyalty and honesty has stood up more easily than in others. There are many times where staying true to your word and remaining loyal reap the deserved rewards. There are also times where it can bite you right in the arse.

Thank God this wasn't one of those times.

♦

I was standing in front of the Roger Millward Stand and looking out over the pitch at Craven Park. It was covered in frost and not fit for post Christmas training. The speedway track was gone but the ground still looked the same. But there was one big difference. When I arrived here first time around, Hull Kingston Rovers was in National League Two. Now it was Super League and you could feel the buzz about the place.

I'd always promised the chairman, Neil Hudgell, that when Rovers made it to the Super League... if they wanted me I would be the first one to put my hand up. When I first made that promise I didn't realise that it would mean leaving a club like Bradford Bulls to keep it. But you can either talk about honesty and loyalty or you can show that you have it. It was easier for me because I wanted to come. I love this club. It was Rovers that first gave me a chance to play rugby over here, it was Rovers that put its arm around me and changed my life more than I could ever have imagined. And now it was payback time.

I don't think it was simply a case of my heart ruling my head. I'd seen the team playing great rugby in 2006 and wanted to be a part of the return. I wanted to play in the games against Hull FC and see the fans who had become friends. I had no doubts that I had made the right decision. Well, at least that was on January 2nd.

All the time that I was away I always supported Rovers, watching them whenever I could. It's my favourite club in the whole world and I'm definitely a fan as much as a player. So there was no way that I was going to miss the decisive game with Widnes that saw them get promoted in 2006. Jo wanted to watch it as well and so did my son Elliott, so as Jo was heavily pregnant we all stayed at home in Huddersfield to watch it on TV.

Now Jo has never been the sort of wife who always wants to be at the game. There's a big difference between rugby players' partners and footballers 'WAGs'. Jo has never been on Big Brother but if she was I wouldn't have to tell my mates not to watch it! She has never released her own record, had a fight at a funeral or launched a perfume. But she has heard of Mother Theresa, can tie her own shoelaces and her hair is all her own. Best of all we support each other and we share everything together. Jo has been my best friend and my strength through eleven years of ups and downs. We met in Hull and her parents Paul and Stephanie still live there, so it was no surprise that she was interested in this game. But she seemed really interested. I mean really interested. She even hushed me when the teams were read out. Now living with someone who is six months pregnant you learn to take things in your stride. So I checked the tray of snacks for a blancmange and pork scratching combo and settled down.

We said that we wouldn't move for the whole game, so we got together enough drinks to last the afternoon, water for Jo of course, and we sat down. Thank God we had a downstairs toilet!

I can remember it was a warm and sunny day. Perfect for being outside I thought, as I sat next to Jo and her big fat tummy.

We couldn't have known how well Rovers would play. They started really strongly and just got better. They showed great passion and desire. Their explosive start took the wind out of Widnes and it wasn't a game where you worry that they're getting closer and closer. They were just overpowered.

As the game went on Jo held my hand, and although we didn't talk about it straight away, we both knew it was a big day.

Suddenly, many conversations I'd had with Neil Hudgell ran through my mind. I can remember him saying to me, when I was at Huddersfield:

"When I become Chairman Stan, the first job I'm going to do is bring you back here. You'll be my first signing."

I'm sure he actually became Chairman in 2004 so he got that one wrong! It started as a joke I think, but Neil is a persistent bugger. When I first met him I didn't know he was a solicitor, but as the years rolled on that proved to be useful on a number of occasions! I still don't have a UK driving licence. When I learnt to drive there were only about ten cars a day passing through our village and there is some confusion over whether my PNG licence is valid in the UK. But no one knows that apart from me and Neil. And I'm determined to keep it that way.

Anyway, every time I went to his office over the last year, he always said to me:

"Do you realise you're coming back here?"

And he'd shove a contract on the desk and say:

"Just sign this, just there, I just need a signature just leave it there."

I'm sure that if I'd signed it - that would have been a done deal at any time. I told Neil that I would love to come back, and if Rovers got in the Super League of course I'd be there. But I wouldn't come just for the sake of it. Only if I was good enough and only if I could make a difference. I didn't want to be one of those players who go to a club to finish their career off. I wanted to go back to Hull to challenge.

♦

As we sat on the settee watching the game, Jo and I knew that it was important to both of us. Jo had never seen me sit still for forty minutes, and I can't tell you the strain on my bladder. And for my part, I knew that Jo had only been to twenty or thirty games in her life. But this one was special.

At the final whistle Jo started shouting, Elliott was jumping around – I don't know if he knew why. But I now know what was happening in Jo's mind. She was pregnant and the baby was coming in January. She wanted to get back to her Mum and Dad in Hull … and what better way to go back. To Jo her Mum and Dad are so precious, they are wonderful people.

But she never told me how much she wanted to go home. She knew that I was half way through a two year contract at Bradford Bulls and I was over thirty. I know you won't believe that. But Bradford is such a big club and in my first year there I was really enjoying myself, I was having a fantastic time playing footy at a great club. For me it felt like I was sixteen years old again, having such a challenge playing for a team like Bradford. And as far as Jo was concerned I was looking forward to my second year, which I was. That was, until Rovers were promoted.

I hadn't told Jo of the conversations I'd had with Neil, and so at that very moment both of us were excited for different reasons, without either of us knowing how each other really felt!

There were three parts of me telling me what I should do - my mind, my body and my heart. The first two were whispering 'stay'. The third was shouting something else.

Jo is such a strong and loving partner. She had been living away from home for nearly five years and wanted to go back. But she wanted the best for me and so her mind told her that we should stay.

But I think her heart agreed with mine.

We sat hugging with tears in our eyes and I still don't know whether we quite knew what would happen next. Elliott was still jumping around and he started shouting:
"We're going back to Hull, we're going back!"

At that moment Elliott had yelled out just what both Jo and I would have done, if we had talked about what we really wanted before the match had started. But maybe if we had known how much we all wanted to go, the match would have been unbearable.

Jo was so happy when I told her I had made my decision to go back to Hull, even though it meant leaving the best team I'd played for. And Jo had been teaching in Batley and she too was enjoying her work more than ever. Teaching is a job that needs stacks of commitment and these days it's incredibly hard. I have seen Jo come home from work crying, feeling so much stress. But in Batley she was really enjoying herself. And I had never seen her so happy in her work. She was getting up in the morning with a smile on her face, and coming home talking about the kids and what she'd done. I loved seeing how happy she was. But the thing was that the pull for both of us to go back to Hull was too great to resist. For the two of us to give up our dream jobs and be so pleased to do it tells you what we had in our hearts.

◆

The next day I went to see Steve McNamara the Bradford coach. I'd known Steve a long time and we'd become good friends. And I knew he'd be ready to have a go at me because he was from Hull, and black and white through and through. I remember walking into his office to see his cheeky smile and he said:

"Hey Stan, your boys have done it. We going to play to play Rovers next year."

He looked at me and could see something in my eyes, and he scratched his head:

"Oh come on, don't give me a headache Stanley."

I had tried all night to work out the best way to tell Steve that I wanted to leave. But this wasn't going to be easy. So I made it as easy as I could by blaming Jo!

"Mate, Jo's pregnant and she's giving up work. She wants to go home and I have to go to Hull."

But Steve wasn't going to give up easily. He shrugged his shoulders:

"It's not that simple Stan. You've signed a contract and you're only half way through it. You're a Bradford player."

I wasn't happy. Jo and I had made up our minds, and now that we'd done that we were desperate to go home. But I knew that Bradford had my contract and they had all the power. I am convinced that the only reason they eventually let me go was that Steve and I had spent two and a half years at Huddersfield together and he understood me more than most. We passed many hours driving up and down the motorway talking about family and home all the time. What we would do after rugby and stuff like that. He knew that I'd started my career at Rovers and that's where I always wanted to end it.

It helped that Steve knew all this. It also helped that Bradford wanted to sign David Solomona from Wakefield and they needed to release some funds! So when Steve called me to say that they would release me from my contract, our dream was nearer to becoming reality.

But in all the excitement the cold, harsh truth of my professional decision had hit home. I was leaving a top four club to go to a team that might stay up, and might go down. Although I later had my doubts, it was always the right thing to do.

I had some great times down at Bradford and we had been happy in our home at Milnsbridge. I particularly loved fishing in the river near our home; a pastime I always say is my favourite hobby. As a kid in Goroka, we didn't have many fish up in the mountains, but in the little creeks there were tadpoles. We went catching the tadpoles and put them in jars to take to school, where we watched them and learnt about how they turned into frogs. I was hooked. Then, we were all excited to discover that there was a river nearby where the local council was throwing in trout. We'd spend hour after hour there, using rods that we made by tying a piece of string to a stick and making a hook out of barbed wire. I love fish. I'm fascinated by the beauty of fish. And the most relaxing thing I do is to spend my day fishing. There's nothing I enjoyed more on a summer day in Milnsbridge than putting my wellies on, packing my bag with sandwiches and walking to Slaithwaite for a days fishing. If it started raining, I'd just walk up to the road and call in to the pub for a couple of pints, then get a bus back home. Perfect.

Back in 1996 when I first arrived in Hull they did a players profile in the programme, and when they asked what my hobby was I said it was fishing. Before I knew it a fishing shop on Holderness Road called Everett's had sponsored me. I'd sort of exaggerated my hobby a bit. What Everett's didn't know of course was that my fishing triumphs to date numbered one sick trout and forty three tadpoles! So they gave me about £500 worth of gear. Two rods and a full set of waterproofs. I'd never seen anything like it before. I could handle a stick and string, albeit with modest success but I had no idea how to use a rod… or what the waterproofs were for. I stored them in my flat and thought no more about it.

Then I noticed a young lad across the street who'd set off every weekend with all his stuff. I recognised the shape of his bag. It was a fishing rod! So one day I asked him where he was going. And when I told him I had some fishing equipment he said he'd take me along. He never wore waterproofs but even so I was sure he'd know how to work my rod. Brilliant!

There were many things that excited me when I first arrived in England but few more so than this. In the cool misty morning, we stood very still, man versus nature, as men had stood for centuries before us. Not in East Park admittedly but that didn't matter. I was bursting with anticipation. My young friend started to unpack his tackle, ready for the battle ahead. I took my rod out of its case. How I wished I'd done that at home so that it wouldn't have taken me so long to find the handle! My companion gave me a quizzical look.

"You do know how to use it don't you?"

"Yeah, yeah, yeah" I lied.

After all, how difficult could it be? Maybe it's a bit more complex than a stick and string, but surely you use it the same way. Then doubts started to creep in to my mind. In my short time in England I had seen a naked chef with clothes on, eaten a pasty barm, and witnessed a room full of people dancing to a 'birdie song'. These were strange people indeed, but what else can you do with a fishing rod? Luckily, encouragement was on its way.

"It's all in the cast. Throw it as far as you can, but make sure you look behind you first."

I must admit I was pleased to get this advice from someone who had the calm assurance of a man who knew what he was doing. So I followed his instructions to the letter. Well nearly. I wasn't quite sure what he meant by the cast, but anyway I threw it as far as I could. The whole bloody rod! Like a short Tessa Sanderson in a cagoule, I was magnificent. But I didn't get the reaction I expected:

"NOOOO! What are you doing?"

I realised immediately that I shouldn't have done that. As my friend rowed out to retrieve my £60 fishing rod, I was sort of glad that the manager at Everett's wasn't there. But I hadn't got away with it entirely. I didn't realise that my new fishing friend, Matty Brooks, was a rugby player, who happened to be playing for Bradford when I arrived there ten years later. He'd already told all the lads at Bradford about the fishing story, so they couldn't wait to tell it again. And again. Of course I had to tell Matty that I was really good at it now. I could hold on to the rod and everything!

♦

After Jo's birthday, I went to see my family in PNG as I always do in the close season. And it was while I was hanging around at Dubai airport that I received a text from Neil telling me that the deal had gone through. I was a Hull KR player again. I telephoned Jo at home and she started to plan for our future back in Hull. With our new baby on the way it seemed that life couldn't get any better. And after finding out all the news from Mum and my two brothers in Goroka, I couldn't wait to get back to my UK home to be with Jo.

We had lots to do over the next couple of months, planning the move back to Hull and preparing for our new arrival. There was always something that needed to be done and we had little chance to slow down. We took the opportunity to relax whenever we could, and sometimes had a quiet night just watching the telly. I love sport and so I never give up the chance to watch it whenever I can. I really enjoy boxing and on the 9th December there was a fight that I had been looking forward to. It promised to be a great night of entertainment. But it turned out to be a night I will never forget as long as I live.

By 1-30 in the morning I was all set up and raring to go. Armed with a bottle of wine, a family bag of Walkers Sensations and the remote control... I was ready for action.

It was the night of Audley Harrison's British Heavyweight bout with Danny Williams, scheduled for 3 am and I just couldn't wait. Jo was safely tucked up in bed. She'd been a bit tired after a busy day and had gone up at ten. She had spent the day shopping, and when she came home we did some more packing. I'd been throwing bin bags full of stuff down from the loft and Jo had been catching and sorting them. I wasn't surprised that she wanted an early night. But as I settled down I heard Jo call out so I ran upstairs:

"Honey is everything ok?"

I didn't quite get the answer I was expecting:

"Stan, don't panic… but I think my waters might be breaking."

Hmmm. Well I'm no expert on the workings of the female body. I'm not completely sure how mine works sometimes. But what I do know is what a strong woman Jo is. She has been my 'rock' from the day we met, and when it comes to matters at home she's always in control. Always.

Also I'm ashamed to say that there was a small part of me that couldn't believe that Jo's waters were about to break one hour before the big fight!

But she did look a little concerned so after a nervous peep under the quilt I reassured her as only a bloke can:

"No I'm sure you're fine. Try to get some sleep… it should be alright."

I gave her a kiss, dimmed the lights again and went downstairs.   Back in front of the telly the excitement was growing with just one more fight before the main event. So I poured myself a glass of wine, opened the crisps and put my feet up. Life doesn't often get better than this.

'Let's get ready to rumbaaaal!'

But then a terrifying scream that went right through my body filled the house. I showered myself in red wine and crisps. It was more terrifying than anything I'd ever heard in the rainforest. And it was the nearest thing to the noise a piglet makes when it's attacked by a python. It came from upstairs:

"STAN!"

That's not to say that I'd ever heard a piglet scream my name when it was attacked, but it gives you an idea of the noise. It was of course Jo. Hardly surprisingly, it turns out that my earlier diagnosis that 'everything's fine' was as crap as my first attempt at fishing:

"Stan, we've got to go. Now!"

So we grabbed a bag and drove straight to the hospital. The nurse and doctor that saw us asked what had happened. And when I said that Jo thought the waters may be broken, this time no one said: 'No I'm sure you're fine – try to get some sleep'. But then no one asked me, thank God!

It became clear that it might take a day or two, so Jo was given some tablets to help her relax and we settled in for the night. While I sat there, musing that it's a good thing that I'm a rugby player and not a midwife, and before either Harrison or Williams had connected with a meaningful shot … little Leo popped out.

Now Jo never swears, her family never swears. Whenever I go round to their house I always mind my language. But while Leo was making his way into the world she was either very sore, or hadn't forgiven me for my wrong appraisal of the situation at home.

Leo had never heard such language! But then he hadn't heard much of anything. He was six weeks premature and tiny. I could hold him in one hand.

And now Jo was fine.

I had already rung her parents and they drove all the way from Hull to arrive minutes after Leo was born.

♦

He was so little that he was placed in an incubator and we couldn't take him home. Jo had a shower, got cleaned up and we got ready to go home. In all my life and throughout my career, I had never felt so proud of anyone. That was the hardest thing that Jo had ever had to do. And as always, she did it in a way that made me feel that everything was going to be ok. If I had gone through what Jo had, I don't think I would have been able to smile. Or sit down for that matter.

The next two weeks passed in a bit of a haze. We went in to see Leo every day. I was getting knackered because I was training with Rovers and then meeting Jo at the hospital. All this time we were loading up all of our belongings into a van and moving bit by bit. The hardest thing was to go into the hospital, see Leo, wash your hands and then leave him there. Well that was the hardest thing for me because I didn't have to use a breast pump. But Jo was sure that Leo was growing nicely and doing well and so we hoped that he might be home for Christmas. But Christmas came sooner than we expected and it didn't happen.

Christmas for us always meant a trip up to Hull to Paul and Stephanie's home. And this year wasn't going to be any different as we'd expected Leo to arrive in January. They are such warm people and wonderful hosts, the day is always entertaining and I looked forward to it every year. Not least because Stephanie's a great cook and she still thinks I'm a growing lad! I'd almost resigned myself to a chicken chowmein from the Lucky Star for Christmas dinner when we got some great news. The only thing that could have beaten it would have been Leo coming home but this ran a fantastic second.

With all the stiff upper lip and 'never say die' spirit that had won two world wars and recovered from the 2006 Eurovision Song Contest, Stephanie and Paul won the day. If we couldn't go to Christmas Dinner, then Christmas Dinner would come to us! They drove all the way to Huddersfield with a car full of turkey, sausages, sprouts, cheese and everything else you would want. That's one thing I like about the British weather, you can leave food in your car for days without it growing... or moving! Stephanie swept into the kitchen and Paul smiled cheerily. Jo's sister and her husband arrived and Christmas had come. Then we all went down to the hospital to wish Leo a Happy Christmas. But the nurses wouldn't allow us all to go in together so we went in to see the little chap two at a time and then went home for dinner. It was a lovely day, but after dinner it didn't seem quite right. Leo should have been with us.

So Jo and I went back to the hospital. Leo came home the day after Boxing Day and it's great to see him now holding his own. But that was one hell of an experience for us all to go through.

♦

Everyone at Craven Park was up for the start of the season. And for me, the day that I had dreamed of had finally come. I went to the ground and looked around. In the changing room I could see my seat and some of the paintwork was still the same as when I had left. I looked in the boot room and could see the little stool where I used to sit on a Monday and help the old kit man John McLane. I was home again. But some things had changed for sure. We were newly promoted to the Super League, and with a squad that had the guts and ability to stay there. There were some great players there when I arrived, James Webster, Mick Vella, Ben Cockayne.....we had strength right through the team. We were determined to make a good start. And we did. When I say we, I was there to support, but didn't catch a footy throughout the whole of February!

I'd injured my knee playing in the World Club Championship the year before, and after our pre season training I went straight into an operation as soon as I got home. So I always knew that I'd struggle to make the first fixture, at home to Wakefield live on Sky. The ground was bouncing to the tune of 'Red Red Robin'. And we got the result we desperately wanted to get points on the board. Gareth Morton kicked three goals and we won it 14-9. The team had worked their bollocks off and sweat blood to get this result so we knew this would be a tough year, but we also knew that we could survive.

I had eight days to get fit for the next game. It was a dream fixture for me. It was away at Huddersfield, where I had played some of my best footy for four years. From the moment the fixture list came out, I starting dreaming of returning there with the Rovers, going through the posts and scoring a somersault try in front of the screaming fans. Yes! I couldn't wait.

But excitement turned to frustration. I was dreaming after all, and I had to sit that one out too. It was great to see the lads pick up another two points but I had to be patient and bide my time.

My time came just two weeks later. I said when I came back to Rovers that I wanted to challenge and pit myself against the best. So I had nowhere to hide when that chance came at the mighty Wigan. It was a cold Friday night and over 15,000 pie filled fans turned out to see Wigan give us a stuffing. I'd been on coaches driving away from Wigan many a time, heads down and sulking after losing badly. And I can't deny that I wasn't looking forward to going through that again. In a way that's what spurred me and the rest of the team on. Fear of failure can be a very powerful tool. Before every match I always write on my hand, 'You're from PNG –don't forget'. I love my home country, but I always thank God for the chance I got to play in England, and I can never take for granted everything I have and owe to the game. The whole team ran out on to the field with that fire in its belly and spurred on by the pastry spattered scorn that the home fans heaped on us. Don't get me wrong, Wigan is a club I admire tremendously, but rival fans can sometimes get you going as much as your own.

The other sixteen boys with me that day put on a brilliant, wonderful show. Byron Ford was like shit off a shovel and they just couldn't handle him as we won 26-16! Radio Humberside covered the match and some diehard Rovers supporters later told me that they were gutted they hadn't made the trip. The two thousand that had left work early to be there enjoyed every single second of it. Just three years before they had watched Rovers get slaughtered by Batley in front of just over 1,000 people. This was dreamland. They jumped up screaming and hugging each other.

Back in the dressing room we went crazy, banging on the walls. We're not bad lads but there's no doubt the Wigan boys could hear us. What a way for me to come back for my first game. And at Wigan!

♦

But we soon found out that things were going to get tougher and tougher as the season went on. Sure there were highlights, beating Leeds and even better, Hull F.C. at the Millennium Stadium. But we were on the end of some horrible thrashings from Saints and Warrington Wolves. More worryingly, we lost to Wakefield, Harlequins and Catalans all of who we knew would be at the bottom end. Often, we made a good start to a game but lost our lead. I don't think it was lack of fitness, just inexperience from time to time. We made some bad decisions. The most disappointing thing is that throughout 2007, we were the best vocally supported team in the league, but we won more games away from home than at Craven Park.

The worst day of all was at home to Salford in April. This was a must win game and we had to hold our nerve. Not least Justin Morgan our coach. Now Justin is a great kid. He's always ready to tell you that he's the youngest coach in the Super League by miles….but I know there's a small part of him that worries that he's older than me. But he has developed a smooth image and a calm head. A man of culture, he enjoys a fine Cuban cigar from time to time. Unusual for a thirty two year old you may think, but maybe it's an Australian thing. Also Justin has the largest and most outlandish collection of shoes I've ever seen. He has a different pair for every game, sometimes made out of crocodile, sometimes snakeskin, it's all a bit weird.

At half time in the Salford game we were glad he wasn't wearing steel toecaps! We had conceded three tries in the first seven minutes. We'd been caught with our pants down and just couldn't recover in time. That was our lowest moment. It was really hurting me. This was a club that I came back to because I love it, and losing was something I found hard to stomach. I had come to back to Rovers for a dream end to my career, not a bloody nightmare. We knew we were in the shit and it would take an elephant size spade to dig us out.

We dug with all our collective might, picking up vital wins, including a battle in Salford to give ourselves a chance. And with three games to go survival was in our own hands. But the last two games of the season were against Wigan and Huddersfield, so we couldn't rely on winning points there. But on the 2nd of September we had a chance. With one small complication....we were going to the K.C. Stadium for the derby. No pressure there then!

From the moment that Rovers were promoted in 2006, the whole city had a lift. Now boasting two Super League clubs, and with four derby matches to look forward to, there was an excitement around that I certainly hadn't seen before. But with the fervour comes rivalry. The Rovers fans had suffered jokes and jibes for too long as F.C. had moved to a brand new stadium and had been a strong top flight club. Promotion brought no ending to the cracks though, with many a Hull F.C. fan 'looking forward to eight easy points this year'. I still get stick from some F.C. fans but you can't let it get to you. And we had already beaten them once this season. We just had to do it again.

For some of our team this was the most pressure they had felt in the game. They didn't have much experience of pressure footy ...real 'do or die' games. The atmosphere at the K.C. was electric, the fans were packed in and there was a sea of black and white, singing and cheering. It was a lovely sunny day and it was the kind of moment that gives you goose bumps. I remember looking at our fans behind the goal and wondering what was going on in their minds, what was going on in the Board's minds and what was going on in the Chairman's mind? Not to mention his wife! Jo Hudgell is as passionate a fan as Neil and she had been to hell and back this season. It was for those people, every Rovers fan on the end, and every one at home listening to the radio and praying, everyone who had heard, 'thanks for the eight points this year' that we had to do or die.

I started on the bench, and suddenly felt more nervous than I can remember. F.C. needed to win to stay in the play offs so they had even more incentive than simply sending us down. But the lads started with such composure, and all the collective strength and spirit that we had shown at Wigan exactly six months before rose again. We moved into a good lead and just needed to hold firm. But there was always the spectre of disaster there. Just over a month ago, Warrington scored sixty against us and I tried not to think the unthinkable. I looked at the scribble on my hand. I couldn't read it but that didn't matter.

Then with about fifteen minutes to go I could sense that we were going to do it. Everyone was fighting for their lives. I think we were about 28-6 ahead and surely we'd done enough. I couldn't have hoped for what was about to happen next.

I collected the ball the ball about twenty metres out. I saw some kid come for me, so I jumped over him, went sideways and then looked up. I could see the try line straight ahead and I'm sure I could hear Justin shout, 'run Stanley'! Now Justin's coaching is often more sophisticated than that, but this was not a time for daydreaming!

As I went over the line, four thousand Rovers fans went completely crazy. The end just erupted. People were jumping up and down, grabbing and shaking each other. It was an explosion of red and white. Everyone was shouting and screaming and I just wanted to be in there with them.

So I jumped over the advertising boards and ran towards them. I screwed up my face, clenched my fists and let out a mighty yell. The fans could see exactly what this meant to me, the passion I still have and my love for the club. We'd done it ….and here of all places.

But what nobody realised was the amount of pain I was in. I know I'm getting older, but jumping over the hoardings I had cracked my dodgy knee on the Kentucky Fried Chicken advert and I was in agony!

As I limped over towards the touchline signalling that I was hurt, I was met by a beaming Justin who said:

"No way Stan, you stay on there. We haven't won yet."

I gave him a big hug anyway because at that moment I knew we were safe. I guess I didn't care whether I was on or off. This was the end of our first season in the Super League and we'd just beaten Hull 42-6 at their own ground to stay up

Wake me up someone.

2

Bird Of Paradise

Pre 1978
Goroka

Have you ever thought what it would be like to go from a tropical island in the South Pacific all the way to Hull to play rugby? It's rather like if you guys went to the North Pole for a game, but much further. It would freeze every part of your aching body. In fact your penis would disappear completely and when nature called you'd have to sit on the toilet!

Clearly this isn't something I'd admit to 1,200 hairy miners in Dewsbury on a Friday night in February, but it's true. And rugby league isn't the sort of game where you can wear gloves and tights, let alone a duffel coat and woolly hat. As for trying to find your vital organ, just forget it. I've often wondered how people get up to nooky on skiing holidays. And what kind of lunatic would go on a holiday where everything is frozen in any case?

In Hull you can wear an overcoat in July without anyone thinking you're up to no good, and as soon as the sun comes out everyone rushes to Bridlington to sit on the front...eating ice cream and shivering. For sure, the impact of global warming has prompted people to scrape last year's remains off the barbeque in May, and now there are mosquitoes in Kent. But it's still a bit cold. Imagine lighting up a barbeque and throwing on the sausages back in the North Pole and you'll have some idea how I felt when I first arrived.

I had come from a land where the heat is sometimes unbearable. A place where I had never seen an electric heater let alone thermal underwear. But that isn't the only difference between England and Papua New Guinea. Let me tell you about my homeland.

PNG is a wonderful, wonderful place, off the north coast of Australia and south east of Asia. It has the most incredible beauty, spectacular landscapes and amazing wildlife. Sometimes it can be frightening. And danger is never too far away, whether from the land, animals or man. But more than anything, it is in my heart. I love it just as much as you love your home town. And I have spent two thirds of my life there. All my blood family live in PNG, and while Jo and I have often talked about holidaying in Europe or the USA … I go to my homeland every year. To see my two mums.

♦

Human remains have been found in Papua New Guinea dating back 50,000 years. Archaeologists have tried to determine what the discovered inhabitants were doing at the point of death but it may have been the conga.

It seems that everything was quiet for the next 45,000 years, but then traders from South East Asia came to hunt the iconic creature of our country -the bird of paradise. The plumes of the bird, with all the colours of the rainbow, were sold at a high price and were a symbol of prosperity and vibrancy.

There are many species of the beautiful bird of paradise, but it is only found in New Guinea, and the northern tip of Australia. It is our bird of paradise, and the symbol of the national rugby team… the Kumuls.

PNG is bigger than England and most of it is covered by untamed rainforest. It is also mountainous. The highest point is almost 15,000 feet high on Mount Wilhelm, and we often have volcanic eruptions and earthquakes, as well as tsunamis. It is very hard to connect settlements, towns and cities by road and so there are 578 airstrips. 557 of them are unpaved so I guess you could call them long fields. If you look right in the centre of the country in the dense mountain area, you'll find my home town of Goroka.

The population of PNG is growing really quickly. When I left in 1996 it was around three million but I think it's twice that now. Back home there is no controlled contraception and, in tradition, men usually have two or three wives. But things are starting to change. Having more than one wife is becoming less common and women are getting more respect. Over the last few years we have tried, through rugby league, to change attitudes and show that women should have meaningful rights. And that they have an equal share of responsibility and worth as men. You wouldn't see that in Batley would you? Certainly not in the Working Men's Club! But it's true. The only way to get a social message across in PNG is by rugby league clubs working with the government. Just imagine a collection of Premier League soccer players in the UK fronting a campaign of respect for women. Hmmm, maybe not!

And getting messages over in PNG can be difficult. After all we have over 800 different languages, one for every 3,500 people when I lived there! You can sit in a pub with your mate and not understand a word anyone else is saying. Mind you, you could go from Hull to Newcastle and have exactly the same problem, but at least in the UK words are spelt the same even if they sound different.

So rugby has a massive voice. We play lots of sports in PNG - soccer, cricket, basketball. But rugby league is like football is over here. It's a religion and people go crazy about it. It is often said that in many ways rugby league has replaced tribal warfare. Supporters often fight and I know people who have died at a game. I knew them personally because unlike football in the UK, the players are on a level with the fans. Sure they are stars but they're not out of reach. When I first played professionally in 1992 I was paid 75 Kina a week ... about £20! And we didn't have stadiums like we know here. There was one big ground, the Royd Robson Oval at Port Moresby, but most stadiums were just built into a clearing surrounded by trees.

At our stadium in my home town of Goroka we had stands, with benches instead of seats and they'd hold maybe 1,500, but a lot more than that would watch the game. Some guys who were locked out would get angry and fight, but others would find ways to see the match. The ground was in a sort of well and there was plenty of room on the surrounding hill to watch. Guys would drive their Lorries right up to the stadium fence and stand on the roofs. And there were supporters we called the 'branch managers'. Not because they were in charge of a group of fans, but because they could climb up coconut trees and hold on for eighty minutes! Their goal celebrations were obviously restricted, apart from the very stupid ones. So it was always a good idea if you were underneath a branch manager to see if he'd got his shirt on the right way round.

But there have been many tragedies. One of the worst was at Goroka in 1994 when I saw four kids watching the game from a mango tree. The branch they were sat on broke and they all fell. One of them died instantly when he hit the concrete ground below. A few of us from the team went to his funeral to show our respect and grief, and no matter how used you think we are to the experience of early death, the value of life becomes much clearer when it is lost.

Rugby fans are so crazy back home. They can be very nasty and they just want to win at all costs. Especially up in the highlands they can be really violent. And they always look for revenge. If one of their fans was killed at a match then they would look to get 'an eye for an eye' at the next opportunity. Sometimes when there was only one road away from the stadium they would block the road after the game and stop everyone to loot the cars. The coastal teams were not as bad though and we always believed that was because 'white man came from the sea'. The coastal tribes had education and influence from overseas visitors but we were too far away up in the mountains. We were the last people to see any civilisation! I've played in matches where some fans were fighting right through the game and police were coming in spraying teargas. It doesn't make it any easier playing in a small stadium when there's a policeman waving a teargas gun around like Rambo. It certainly doesn't make you laugh!

So the rugby league stars had a responsibility to say as often as they could: "Look it's just a sport". But actually it was a matter of life and death for some.

I was in a game when Great Britain toured in 1994 and during the match a big fight started. And the English guys really shit their pants. They thought they were going to die. But at least they didn't start singing like the welsh blokes in 'Zulu', otherwise they probably would have.

But the weirdest thing for us in the Kumuls team was when we saw two of the GB players, Ellery Hanley and Roy Powell. We just couldn't believe our eyes. We'd seen Australian guys before who were white and we knew that the English players would be white as well. But these two were black! How could that be? We all looked at each other when they came onto the pitch, and when we'd plucked up the courage we moved towards them slowly. We just wanted to see them up close but they thought we were going to hit them or eat them! They were on the twenty metre line by the time we reached them.

♦

Like I said, Rugby players are idols in New Guinea. And they are often asked by politicians to help promote a message or a policy. If you think Westminster is riddled with sleaze, then you should have a look at our government back home. The thing I love about scandal in England is that everyone, or at least some people, act surprised when a politician is caught doing something naughty. Power does corrupt weak people. But when a government official is accused of taking a bung or dropping his pants on Hampstead Heath, he never smiles and says: 'Oh well, I knew I'd get caught sooner or later.' Never. In a financial scandal you always see supportive colleagues looking straight into the camera and delivering loads of spin, as the central PR machine prepare the guilty man's bosses for a few rounds with Paxman. Or in the case of an embarrassing sexual gaff, the guy poses with his wife who 'is going to stand by him', or he says he was looking for a rare plant in the undergrowth when his trousers got caught on a branch and fell off.

The best example of this is when seven or eight famous politicians all admitted they'd tried soft drugs at University when they were kids. Every single one of them was curious to try it, but didn't like it one bit! Now what's the point of saying that? Are they asking us to believe that out of eight teenagers who smoked a spliff not one of them liked it? Bollocks. What makes politicians so different to everyone else? You'd think that out of eight of them at least one would have enjoyed a puff! It just makes the kids who they're trying to influence think that they're making it all up to look cool. Which of course has the opposite effect.

So on the whole, politics in the UK is very much like a sitcom compared to government activity back home. In PNG there are many political parties. The Prime Minister, Michael Somare, is a member of the Pangu party and he has been in power, apart from a couple of terms, since the country gained independence from Australia in 1975.

The thing you need to know about PNG, is that in terms of natural resources it is one of the richest countries in the world. Three quarters of our exports are oil, copper and gold, and we have cocoa and coffee in huge supply. Now investors are coming over to take wood from our rainforests but that's another story.

In terms of distribution of wealth and material comforts, the people of PNG are among the poorest, it really is a third world country. So where does all the money go?

Politics is a dangerous world and in every election someone gets shot. The rich are getting richer, and the politicians are right in the middle of it all. So at election time the stakes are high. The winners know that there is a big pot of gold and they will get their share. Investment from exports is paid to the government, and they control all the money without having to answer to anyone who doesn't have a gun. Finances are agreed and distributed across the country every three months, and then the money disappears. And in settlements less than ten minutes walk from Goroka there is no electricity or water. Twenty minutes away they don't have roads. Of course, the central government in the capital city, Port Moresby, will have received a piece of paper from Goroka saying that everyone now has electricity and water and the job is done!

I keep getting asked to get into politics over there but I don't want to. When I go there on holiday I want to see my family, help people in the village and play rugby with the kids. Politics is a definite 'no' for me. When you play rugby you want to be friends to everyone. My desk mate from my primary school, Thomson Lavakave is the MP for Goroka. He's fighting a court battle with the previous MP at the moment. It seems that some ballot boxes might have gone missing, but that happens in every election anyway, just like in Florida…. allegedly. I want to go and see him but I can't because people would think I was getting involved. It's very sad and I feel sorry.

So that's why I try to help people back in the villages to do what they always used to. Look after the land and plant vegetables and make your money that way. Villages are very different from towns and cities and you should stay there if you can. In a village you can grow your vegetables, get them out of the ground and you have your food. In a city to get food you need money, and where are you going to get that from? You might have to steal. Agriculture still gives a livelihood to 85 percent of the population and never gets anyone shot!

In recent years we have seen investors come in for logging and you can see the rainforest being chopped down in some places. I know one landowner who did a deal with the investors. They built him a fabulous house from his own logs and gave him a nice car. He had never had such luxury. But he didn't think about what he was doing. He gave the investors lots and lots of logging and soon they were making millions chopping down the trees. It makes me very angry. But what can I do?

You have to remember that Papua New Guinea is a great country, a very beautiful country with a rich culture. You can climb up into the mountains and see the wonderful wildlife in the rainforest, or go to the beach in a real tropical paradise. And in any case you will find corruption wherever you find money, no matter where in the world you are.

♦

It's summer nearly all year round and it's so, so hot. I felt lucky because up in the mountains it's really hot but it's not humid. Down at the coast it's very sticky. And like any tropical country when it rains, it really rains. The wet season is from December to February and sometimes we have continuous rain, morning to noon and night, day after day. I just can't work out how Hull was flooded last summer. In Hull we have a really good drainage system and it didn't rain much at all but it flooded. In a monsoon it rains non-stop for four or five days. Our homes were built of wood and on the soil, so when water came into the house we all rushed out with spades to dig the drain deeper. I think that's what you call a coordinated flood defence.

My grandfather always knew when it was going to rain by watching an orchid. He'd look at an orchid, narrow his eyes and say, 'Hmmm, it's going to rain.' We'd all laugh and then sure enough, within an hour we'd be drenched. Then he'd look at another orchid and say, 'Well now, it's going to be sunny', and we'd be sweltering all day. It was so funny. I often think if the British Meteorological Centre had asked my grandfather to check his orchid last summer, they could have evacuated Tewkesbury in good time. But then floating down the high street on a settee looks quite good fun to me.

Now and then we'd have a deluge. One minute it was a beautiful sunny day, and then suddenly the rain would come. So many bridges have simply been washed away that the Australian government has granted a fund to build new ones. So now they just build cheap bridges and replace them every two or three years!

When we were kids we used to love rain because it gave us a chance to go sledging. If you hollow out the trunk of a banana tree, and attach two sticks to the sides, you can sledge down the mud banks in the mountains all day long. Or you can just use a bin. We had great fun and we used to really fly. It's very dirty but not cold.

If you ever watch the Discovery channel you're sure to have seen some of the wildlife in New Guinea. I tell my friends over here that you have to go sometime. Seeing is believing. We have butterflies that are bigger than kangaroos! Before you have nightmares they're not six foot tall, but the bird wing butterfly is enormous and it can certainly give you a surprise. And PNG is the home of the tiny tree kangaroo. So there you go.

And of course there are the birds of paradise, the kumuls. They are the nation's pride and joy and our country's emblem. So you can see we like them. There are so many with such an array of beautiful colours, but we have to take care of them. Some species are now getting close to extinction. The plumes are still a high currency, not only for tribesmen, but also for overseas traders. And the steady annihilation of the rainforest is a big threat.

Throughout my life I have never been afraid of anything. That is apart from snakes. They give me the willies. It's not the reason I left the country but I don't miss them one bit. I'd stick my head in anywhere, withstand serious pain and I'd even open the door to a Jehovah's witness. Sure, there are one or two rugby players that I'd like to stay away from on the field, like Iafeta Paleaaesina at Wigan. He's big and when he runs his knees go so high, to me anyway. But you can't get out of the way because you'd look a prick in front of a lot of people. But throw a snake at me and you won't see me for dust. I don't care.

There are over one hundred species of snakes in PNG and they're all shit! The most poisonous ones live down near the coast thank God, which is one reason I'm not a surfing fanatic. There are some really nasty vipers down there. When I've been home doing hospital visits the doctors have told me that they lose almost 3,000 lives a year to snake bites, and those are only the guys who make it to the hospital. Up in the mountains you're more likely to see a tree python. They aren't poisonous but they are big. Every now and then you'd hear that a pig or a wild boar had been killed and eaten by a snake nearby. And when I first got my fear of snakes I knew some pigs that were as big as me!

During the harvesting season I always went to help my family pick coffee down at their plantation. It wasn't that big, about the size of a footy field, but we got a good supply every year. For six months we'd prune the trees and keep them healthy. And then we would pick the coffee berries when they were red and ripe. The whole village would come to help. And I remember one year helping out on a very hot day.

I think I was about six years old and I was small but strong for my age. And I can remember seeing a bunch of beautiful ripe coffee berries that were ready to pick. The best berries are often at the top and they were quite high up so I had to reach to grab the branch and pull it down towards me. The branches bend easily so they never break. I was on my tiptoes, using all my strength and balance to reach the bunch without falling over. But the branch seemed much heavier than usual, so I let go and sat down for a rest. It was near the middle of the day and getting very hot. Maybe it was time to ask Mum when we could eat. We had brought some pork and greens and sweet potato and made a big hole in the ground and cooked them in a pot. We'd been picking for over two hours and my little drum was nearly full of berries and I was hungry. The smell of the stew was good, but Mum was still busy so I'd have to wait.

I looked up at the bunch that I had aimed for, and with my first demonstration of a fighting spirit I decided that I wouldn't be beaten by any stupid branch. I got a better footing, took a firm hold and pulled the branch down to reach my goal.

Then I had the biggest shock of my short life. As I pulled at the branch a huge green python that had been sucking berries from the same bunch lost its grip and fell right on top of me. I let out the loudest scream my lungs could raise:

"AAAAAGH!"

The beast looked at me. But it was nothing like the scene from Jungle Book when Kaa the snake hisses 'trussssst in me' to a wide eyed Mowgli. Trust in me … not bloody likely.

"Aaaaaagh! Get it away from me!"

I ran as fast as I could. God knows where the snake went. I didn't even finish the picking session. From that day on, every time I went picking coffee I took a stick with me to wave around in the tree.

So you can see it's not an entirely irrational fear. I hate them.

♦

On the subject of creepy crawlies we are also blessed with many spiders in PNG. They're absolutely everywhere, particularly up in the rainforest. And they can be quite big. They're usually about the size of a kid's hand, but often a lot bigger, although not as big as a kangaroo, although bigger than some small butterflies. They can be any size really. And we like to eat them. I remember as a kid we used to collect spiders out of the coffee drums and then we'd fry them and eat them. They don't really taste of anything but they're very crispy.

And they liked to eat us as well. Not many of them are poisonous. Just like the snakes, the more poisonous ones live down by the coast. But they can give you a nasty bite. And the bigger the spider the bigger the bite, they can easily make you bleed. But they never worried us. We lived with spiders and we lived with rats. Home wouldn't be home without them.

I love the way some girls, and guys, in the UK are terrified by spiders and they're so tiny over here. Jo is really frightened when she sees one. It's so funny. I'll hear a scream from the bedroom and find Jo standing on the bed pointing at a little spider in the corner that you can hardly see. It's completely crazy. But it's certainly entertaining and spiders can run quite fast too.

When Jo first came over to Papua New Guinea in 1997 I was really excited. Jo was too, but I knew she was worried about the spiders. Her parents were worried about everything, and they didn't know how to ask me about cannibalism without offending! But she came over when I asked her to and has visited with me ever since.

I flew over early and I had been at home in the settlement for a couple of weeks before the day came when Jo was due to arrive. I knew she would be here in four hours or so and I was hopping around. I didn't know what to do with myself. Then I had an idea. You probably think I'm a big kid and the ladies will think I'm a shit. But I went out onto the balcony at the back of my house and reached over to the trees that overlooked the veranda. It just came to me that it would be a great laugh to pull over a string of spider's webs so that all the spiders would come down and be here to greet Jo on her arrival. We'd been going out for a few months by now and I knew she could take a joke. If she screams when she sees a little spider in the bath in Hull, just imagine what she'll do when she sees twenty or thirty, big and hairy, in my house! It'll be brilliant. Don't you think?

Then the phone rang. It was Jo.

"Stan, it's me. Where are you?"

"Well you rang me. Where do you think I am?"

This was not the time for satire as I found out.

"Anyway, where are you?" I asked.

It seemed to me to be a fair question the other way round.

"I'm here. I've arrived. You're supposed to be here to meet me you arse. What am I going to do?"

Oh crap. I'd got the time completely wrong and Jo was in the airport at Port Moresby, a forty five minute flight away. She was here in PNG for the first time and all alone. Not good.

So I ran as fast as I could down to the airport in Goroka and I got there in record time. It's a ten minute run but I got there in nearer five. I was just in time to make a flight. I knew that there were only two a day so this was my only chance. I was already feeling guilty and worrying how Jo was doing in Port Moresby.

When I got to the airport I ran straight in and I saw this lady at the desk who I knew. Surely she'd help me out. But I thought I'd play safe by begging.

"Please, please you have to put me on this flight. I have to get on it. You've got to help me."

"Why what's the panic?" At least it looked like I'd got the level of urgency across.

"It's my girlfriend... she's coming over here and she's already in Port Moresby."

"Well shouldn't you be there to meet her?" My heart sank. This wasn't going the right way. "Stanley, the flights fully booked, and you know there are only two a day, one in the morning and one in the afternoon." I knew. And so urgency quickly turned to desperation.

"Pleeaase. You've got to do something."

Then the lady on the check-in became an angel …. and they offloaded somebody from the plane. The next thing, I saw an angry woman at the desk. She was furious and I could hear her ranting and raving, 'I've had this flight booked for weeks. You can't just get me off the plane like this. Who the hell is so important that they have to take my place… huh…huh?' As you'd expect I hid round the corner. I wondered why they'd picked on her and for a brief moment I felt bad. Then I remembered the mess I was in and I ran towards the plane.

Port Moresby has the biggest airport in PNG. There are two terminals, international and domestic. As soon as we landed I ran across the runway and through the doors where the cargo is offloaded. I knew that was the quickest way and thank God they knew me there; they let me straight through and I got into the arrivals room through the back. If Jo was still there she would have been waiting two hours now and my heart was pumping. Then I saw her. She was looking out of the doors and I walked up behind her.

Jo was so pleased to see me. The moment she turned round she gave me a big slap across the face and immediately burst into tears.

"I've been looking out and everyone looks like you! Everyone's black and they all have short hair! You useless sod!"

Then she gave me the biggest hug I'd ever had. Jo had made it to my home. This was a great moment for both of us. I couldn't wait to show her my village and introduce her to my family. It was going to be a wonderful holiday and I promised Jo that she could now relax and I'd take care of her. There was nothing more to worry about. She could enjoy the beauty and the colour of my fantastic country. Jo was still a bit emotional but I had everything under control. Soon she would be wide eyed with amazement and in love with New Guinea. Then I remembered.

By now, the balcony of my house would be crawling with big, hairy spiders. Shit. Shit, shit, shit, shit, shit. Shit. What a stupid thing to do. And I bet all the stupid spiders have accepted the invitation. Shit. Think of something Stan. I could take Jo to my friend's house and go and clean out. No, after being left alone at the airport for two hours she's not going to buy that, Stupid. Oh well. I'd have to take the gamble. Anything could happen. Jo might think it's funny. Hmmm. I might never see her again. Shit. Should I come clean and tell her what I'd done? No, I didn't think she was quite ready for another bout of idiocy so soon.

So I gambled. And when we arrived home I took Jo straight out onto the balcony….

"Whooaaah Stan! Spiders!"

She ran back in to the house, and I quickly cleared up.
"Jeez Honey. I wonder what brought them in." I lied.

I honestly think Jo was just so exhausted that she didn't have the energy to go crazy. Or even to kill me. That's love for you.

I didn't think this was a good time to tell Jo about the fruit bats. As the sun went down they would appear for certain. The bigger ones would come to eat the bananas. My grandfather used to hate them, because if a bat shoved its nose in your bananas, they'd make a hole and you'd end up with maggots in them. And they could give you a nasty bite. But I thought I'd brush that one under the carpet for the time being.

I could remember as a kid hunting bats with a bow and arrow. Or if we wanted an easier way, we'd go into the bush where the bats were and throw a blanket up in the air to catch them.

◆

For many years in Papua New Guinea, a sign of how wealthy you were was the number of pigs you had. And if you had two wives, you had to look after more pigs. That's an odd kind of pressure I guess... two wives, two houses and twice as many pigs!

And pig management was a skill too. When they were big enough, they'd be thrown out into the bush to run wild. I remember being in the village and seeing my uncle's pig walk past, then my Dad's, then my cousin's. They just seemed to go where they wanted. This seemed a bit risky to me because sometimes pigs were stolen, and sometimes the little ones got lost. But then in the afternoon, the owners would come out of their houses with a bucket of old sweet potato and greens and shout out. All the pigs knew exactly where to go, to their own bucket. Every owner had a slightly different shout that his pigs recognised. But I never understood how a man who had two wives could keep the pigs separated. But I didn't want to ask.

Pigs and chickens provided a lot of our food, together with whatever we could get out of the land. A stew with chicken or pork, greens and coconut milk is much better than fried spider. Often we had a meal of sweet potato and greens with salt and oil, and that was great too. I miss the greens. Over here in the UK you can get broccoli, cabbage and cauliflower but not the green leaves with so many different shades.

And I can't find pumpkin seeds like we had back home. I tried to bring some over one time but they were confiscated at the customs in Australia. The next time when I smuggled them successfully, I planted them in my garden in Hull in January, but by March they were dead because it was too bloody cold!

But the land in PNG provides a living to most of the population. And so we all grew up and learned how to work in the bush and provide for ourselves. There were some people who went to the city to work. We called them 'the working class' which has a different meaning than in the UK. They were paid money for their work and so they could buy potatoes and meat.

My family were completely self sufficient and we did ok. I can remember when I went to primary school I only had three or four pairs of shorts, t-shirts with holes in and one pair of trainers if I was lucky. But we were never hungry. I feel so lucky now, and whenever I go home I always take a load of clothes for the village.

Everyone in my village, which was called Segu, was related by blood. I guess that's still the case. There were 30 or so people there and they were all family. Our homes were built from bush materials and logs and we used bamboo for weaving. We always knew that we were very lucky to be able to use natural resources to build our homes. And we had water nearby. As you walked up to our settlement from Goroka, the stream stopped a few minutes short of home. So we used to take turns to carry containers down to the creek to fill with water and return. It was always one of my goals to somehow get water into our village. We didn't have any electricity either but one thing at a time I suppose. The government didn't seem that bothered.

♦

My mum, Christina, is a strong woman, and she is still held in very high regard in our village. Her parents were chiefs in the village and she too was held in that kind of esteem. At an early age she showed that she had the will and the mind to lead a good life. She worked in the hospital in Goroka and so she could always bring money to the settlement. She was the breadwinner for the whole family and had a lot of responsibility on her shoulders. And because she had the brain to work in the city, she had the opportunity to meet other people, and that's where she met my father. Christina was about nineteen I think when she first saw Robert. And he was an impressive kind of guy. He was well dressed and could speak perfect English. He was a very clever man. He had a top job in sales working for Toyota, and this took him all over the country. He worked with a lot of Americans and so he picked up the English language pretty easily.

Robert knew that he had found his match and they were soon married. I always say that my mum is like a man. I don't mean that in a funny way, but that she has all the strength of a man and commanded the same respect. Not because she was physically powerful, but because she was a great leader, and a great carer. In the village if there was any problem and we all came together, it would be Christina who did all the talking. If someone was ill or died in a nearby village, she would be the first one there to give food or care. She would always work hard and help others whenever she could and so her position in the village gained her more respect by the day. And I think Robert must have misjudged that.

Mum fell pregnant a year later, with yours truly. And it was during the pregnancy that Robert decided it was a good time to take a second wife. This was not right for Christina. It is still common for men to have more than one wife but not in this case. There was, and still is, a very uneven status between men and women, but my mum was unique. I'm very proud of my mum.

The village reacted in fury and Robert was chased away. And I had no idea who he was. I didn't meet him until 32 years later.

Now there is a great amount of confusion and speculation surrounding my date of birth. I'm not sure why there's so much interest and I have been asked to publish my birth certificate in this book. But I don't know where it is. And nobody I ask seems to know either. Suffice to say that it was before 1978. How much before is the question?

But I know the detail. I was born by caesarean operation as that is the way of ninety percent of births in PNG. Of course the first three months of my time are a little foggy, but it was during that time that my life took its first change in direction.

My mum Christina had been looked after by her auntie and uncle, Maul and Kaula. They had been there to help her through the birth and got her back onto her feet as she brought me into the world. They took care of me also, and soon I began to cry whenever Maul passed me back to my mum.

Christina was only 21, full of energy and still with her whole life ahead of her. It might seem strange to some of you, but what happened next made absolute sense to all three of them. Christina passed me over to Maul and Kaula, who from that day on became my mum and dad.

I didn't find out who my mum really was until I was sixteen.

3

Brave New World

1996
Hull Kingston Rovers

Have you ever seen the film 'Cool Runnings'? It's a comedy about the Jamaican bobsleigh team. They went from a tropical Caribbean island to the freezing mountains in Switzerland to compete in the Winter Olympics in 1988. I thought it was a training video and I was taking notes for the first half hour!

At this very moment I wished that I had watched it a bit more attentively as it certainly would have stood me in good stead. But I had to learn by myself. Well not just by myself.

I had just taken the biggest step of my life so far. I had never lived any more than five minutes away from my Mum before and now I was on the other side of the world, in England.

I kept wondering to myself how I had ended up here. Of course I was here to play for Hull Kingston Rovers after they had spotted me representing the PNG Kumuls in the World Cup the year before. But it had all happened so quickly and I wondered what on earth I'd done. When I lived in PNG, I found it hard enough flying to the next city to play and I always wanted to get home to my family as soon as I could. Thank God my friend and team mate John Okul was here with me. Rovers had signed both of us because they probably knew that they wouldn't get one without the other. In all honesty John was the player that they badly wanted, even though I'd done pretty well in the World Cup. But now we were both in the same freezing, wet boat.

Well actually it was a silver Mercedes (and it wasn't wet), driven by the Hull KR chairman Barry Lilley. He had just picked us up from Heathrow airport to take us on the 250 mile trip to Hull. 250 miles! That would take us at least four days for sure, but the car was quite comfy so we could just enjoy the ride and marvel at the beauty of England in February.

But I just looked at John in disbelief when I first saw a row of trees by the road. They had no leaves. They were completely bare. The only time I had seen trees without leaves was during a drought, but it was wet here. And bloody cold. I imagined that the world was coming to an end. What a time for me to come to this country when a natural disaster on this scale was happening.

I was still coming to terms with the death of the forests of England when we had arrived in Hull. I had no idea what the city looked like because it was dark and the car windows were streaming with rain, and the sun drenched rainforests of New Guinea seemed even further away.

The first thing I remember was arriving at Craven Park and we were introduced to some guys (to this day I have no idea who they were), before being taken to a press conference. That was quite short because I couldn't put three words of English together. Come to think of it neither could Fabio Capello at his first press conference as the national soccer coach, but somehow his stretched out to fifty minutes. Apparently the Hull Daily Mail didn't have an interpreter.

The whole world had seemed to have gone crazy. This was certainly different to anything I'd ever known and I didn't know what to expect next. As far as I could see the trees were all dead but no one seemed too worried. I also still couldn't quite believe that we were going to get paid for playing rugby. I never knew that happened anywhere in the world, but it made my decision to come to England seem that bit better.

Then we were taken to our new flat above a launderette just off Holderness Road. I was so exhausted that I just wanted to drop my bags and fall asleep. But at the same time I was really excited getting my own place in my new country. There were two bedrooms in the flat, one up in the loft and one on the ground floor where the kitchen was. John took the downstairs room so up I went.

The place seems pretty humble now but I can remember looking around and thinking that I'd really made it. I had never had a cooker before, or a freezer, or even a power light. Jeez, I couldn't wait to ring home and tell Mum all about it. My bedroom even had a cupboard in it and we had a proper toilet that you could flush. Everything you could ever need or want was under one roof. In the lounge there was a television and a couch. I just couldn't believe my eyes - I was used to sitting on the soil. I was so excited that I just went around the house touching everything. This was a different world for sure and somehow, the dampness and darkness outside had completely disappeared from my mind. I slept really well that night.

◆

The next morning when I woke I remembered where I was as soon as I opened my eyes. The cupboard was still there and I lay in bed for a while looking around the room. It was all real. That day I saw some things that I had only seen at the movies in Goroka. Double Decker buses went past my window and I couldn't believe how many people were walking up Holderness Road at nine o' clock in the morning. I wondered what the rush was and where they were all going. But there was something else that had completely freaked me out.

The first thing I saw when I peeped out from under my duvet was the skylight window in my loft bedroom. But it was covered in white. I leapt out of bed and shouted downstairs:

"John, John.... you've got to see this. It's ice.... there's ice on the window, everything's frozen up!"

We looked out of the window downstairs and sure enough there was ice everywhere. Well it was actually snow, on the tops of the cars, on the paths, on the roof tops. We ran outside and started taking photos of everything we could see. And then we took the film to a Max Spielman shop that was opposite our flat.

We got the pictures developed while we were having breakfast, and when we picked them up I couldn't wait to ring home. I was so excited when I heard my mum's voice and I blurted out that I'd seen some snow and we had some pictures and that we'd send them straight home. Mum didn't seem all that impressed in her voice. I think she was crying and she just asked me if I was alright.

The next day was our first training session at the club. John and I had been given a full set of kit including gloves, woolly hats and heated underwear (how does that work?). We also had the thermal coats that you see guys wearing when they're sat on the bench in winter. And when we stepped out onto the pitch we looked like a pair of Eskimos. We were wearing every item of clothing we had been given and decided that we could only play dressed like that. The rest of the team stood looking at us and most of them had big smiles. I found out straight away that the wind always blows right to left at Craven Park and it was freezing, so I stood on John's right. But the English lads were dressed as if they were going to a barbeque. I can remember thinking 'what the hell am I doing here?'

After running around the pitch for a while and then being clattered by some really big lads in their beachwear, we trudged back to the changing room, not understanding exactly what we'd been working on and still freezing.

Then came the next surprise. As John and I sat shivering in our four layers of thermal clothing, the white boys all took off their clothes and went into the showers with nothing on. Nothing at all, they were completely starkers! Now I'm not a prude by any stretch of the imagination but what the hell were they doing? Back home we never got naked in front of anyone else, well not often, and certainly not in front of other guys. Maybe this was some kind of final ritual to mourn the death of the nation's trees and forests, but in all honesty my new team mates didn't seem at all to be the sensitive types.

John and I followed them into the showers after we'd taken off all our clothes apart from our shorts, and the guys were pointing at us and saying, 'what's in there then boys?' At least I think that's what they were saying. They didn't seem to be the gay types either.

I have to say that the team welcomed us better than we could have hoped for. It's hard to explain how nervous twenty white faces can make you and I didn't know whether they'd want to talk to me. But when we first went into the changing room they had walked straight over to us to shake our hands. We couldn't understand them and they couldn't understand us but we had already started to make friends. Paul Fletcher, one of the best second row forwards I ever played with was there, and he became one of my first friends in the UK. He helped me with my language and stopped me making a fool of myself on many occasions.

But he couldn't be there to help me every minute of the day. And I always say that my proudest achievement throughout my career is not just winning trophies or awards. It is that I managed to travel all the way around the world, to a country where I didn't know the culture or understand the language, to play rugby and be part of a team where we all knew what we were doing. Well most of the time anyway.

There were times early on when I found it difficult to get myself understood on the pitch. I had to give a lot of instructions because I was playing half back and so I had to direct a lot of the play. I tried really hard to listen to what the other guys shouted so that I could copy them. One particular call I struggled with was a move that we often used that was called 'Lucky'. There was a game against Halifax when it all went tits up. We were pressing late on to try to snatch a winner. I knew that this was the moment and so I shouted the call which should have been:

"Two to the fifty – Lucky!"

Apparently it came out as:
"Tududuvivdie - Laki!"

The backs went the wrong way, the move broke down, we conceded a try and our hooker gave me the kind of look you would get if you were juggling salmon with your underpants on your head! There is of course no other way to juggle salmon without looking silly.

Steve Crooks, our coach, took it upon himself to look after me in the early days, and after a cock up like this he'd put his arm round me on the Monday and say:

"Stanley, when you're in Rome do as the Romans do. When you're in PNG, do as you want to do. And when you're in England, do as the English do."

Well that was as clear as a swamp on a foggy day. So I'd just look at him with a serious face and nod. I was sure that if it was important he'd tell me again.

♦

Every day I tried to learn a new word and practise it. And as the days went on it became easier so I kept on trying. And as I have said before I always imagined what I'd be doing if I couldn't play rugby in England - probably picking coffee with snakes dropping on my head. That was a powerful incentive. It still always drives me and gets me going if I need a shove.

Almost everything was new to me when I first arrived in Hull and I was like a kid in a sweet shop. The club even gave me a car, a G-reg Volvo. This was the kind of crazy world I was living in now. It was great to own a car but I couldn't drive and I was too scared to even try. I'd never seen cars move as fast as they did up and down Preston Road so I just left it at the club. I sat in it now and then and worked out how to use the radio. I suppose it was a bit of an expensive radio and not that handy in all honesty, as I couldn't move it. But I liked sitting in it and whenever I needed a lift in I would just ring John McLane, the groundsman, and ask him to come and get me.

I'd never driven a car in my life. In PNG I was given my licence by the police when I played rugby for them, but I had never owned a car so I didn't use the licence. John's a lovely guy but I soon got the impression that he may have been getting a bit fed up with me calling for lifts, so he persuaded me to have a go. Well how difficult could it be? No harder than fishing I'm sure!

After showing me how to turn the car on and turn the wipers off he carefully and slowly gave me my instructions. John was always a thoughtful chap so he had planned my challenge in the middle of the afternoon, away from rush hour. There was no one around in the club car park so this was it, my big moment.

John put his arm round me and said:

"Okay Stan, here you go. Drive out of here, turn left and go straight up Preston Road into Holderness Road and back to the flat. You can't go wrong."

Yes, you can't go wrong. That is of course if a) you had noticed over the past few weeks that Preston Road is a dual carriageway, and b) you had listened to John's instructions. So I kangarooed out of the car park and crept towards Preston Road. Seeing my chance I turned right and made it about fifty metres when a car heading straight for me swerved into the middle so I did too. It's always best to copy what the natives do in this country and you can't go far wrong. I managed to drive over the grass onto the other side in a stylish U-turn. So far so good, it was going well! But then I noticed that the cars that were swerving past me were flashing their lights and people were honking their horns at me. I just thought that they knew me so I started waving at everyone. When I got to the junction I realised I was on the wrong side so I stopped. People were still honking their horns and some were getting out and shouting. So I got out of the car, walked back to the club, gave the keys to John and went home. There was quite a crowd around my car when I walked by so I thought it best to stay on the other side.

I don't think my driving improved too quickly. Our coach at the time, Steve Crooks, still thanks me for all the headaches I gave him. Many times I would get lost and get out of the car to walk to the nearest phone box. I would ring Steve and he'd say, 'What can you see? Can you see any street signs?' And when he'd pinpointed my location he would come out to get me. What a great guy. I have to admit that sometimes I'd get out of my car and ring Steve even before I got lost, because I knew that I probably wouldn't be able to find my way home!

♦

One day John and I drove ourselves to a pub to have lunch. But when we came out we couldn't get the car out of the car park, because we couldn't get it into reverse. We were both pulling at the gear stick with all our strength. I can't imagine what people walking by thought we were doing and the car was making terrible grinding noises. So we went back into the pub to phone Steve. I can't say that he sounded pleased:

"What have you done now?"

"We can't get the car into reverse."

"Listen, just lift the gear stick gently and then slide it in."

"We've already done that."

Steve knew that we hadn't and when he turned up he found us pushing the car backwards and forwards. We'd taken the handbreak off but the wheel had now locked so we still couldn't get out. I don't think he could quite believe his eyes:

"You two idiots! Come on Laurel and Hardy, give me the bloody keys."

With that, he got into the car, turned the engine on and to our utter amazement reversed out:

"Hey thanks Crooksy, how did you do that?"

But Steve had already gone.

My car was sponsored by Ottringham Garage and the guys in there were very good to me, they always managed to fix the car up whatever was wrong. But every time I had a bump I was hoping 'please God, give me a new car.' And the boys at the club were starting to get on my back, saying that I should demand a new car, and I noticed that Paul Fletcher had a brand new one. But I was still a bit shy and I didn't like to ask. After all they had been kind enough to give me my first car anyway. So on the way into the car park one day I drove up the kerb and smashed into the automatic barrier. Jeez, what a mess! John McLane came running out and said that it was a write off for sure. Yes!

At the next home game I was so excited because I knew that I would be presented with my new car, and the public address system announced:

"And a very warm welcome to Ottringham Garage the proud sponsors of Stanley Gene's car."

And then the guy came on the pitch to give me the keys and I realised it was the same car. Somehow they'd managed to bloody well fix it!

♦

My flatmate John could speak better English than me because he had spent the previous year in Australia playing at a feeder club in Canterbury. He also knew more about customs and normal behaviour outside PNG than me and he knew how to act without looking out of place.

Now this may sound funny to you, but back home in New Guinea when mates walk around together, down town, having a chat or whatever, they hold hands. It was normal for you to just hold hands and have a hug as you walked. Really!

One Saturday morning when we were walking down Holderness Road I took hold of his hand, and to my surprise he let it go. So I moved over to give him a cuddle and he kept pushing me away saying:

"Get off Stan, you can't do that man."

He was agitated and I didn't like it one bit. Was he trying to be rude? Was he mad at me for some reason? I was getting really pissed off:

"Hey what's your problem John? Why are you acting like this mate?"

"Stan, if you do that over here they think you're gay!"

"What! Are they all out of their minds?" I hadn't fully integrated at this stage.

"No really mate. They do. If you hold hands they think you're queer. Straight up."

I jumped back as if I'd seen a viper wrapped round John's arm, and looked around me frantically to see who was watching. I got a funny look from an old lady across the street who was tutting, 'bloody poofs', so I guessed he had a point.

I had only ever come across one gay man in PNG, if you get my meaning. There was this old Australian guy who was a shirt sponsor for the police team I played for. At the time we thought he lived with his adopted son. But when we saw them kissing and cuddling it turned out they were a couple. No wonder he left Australia! The local people in Goroka wouldn't accept this kind of thing either. Nowadays when I go home, we see gay guys and lesbians and women wearing short skirts, but not ten years ago.

So we stoned his house and he left.

♦

I thank God that I have never been hungry in my life, and that wasn't about to change now that I was in Hull. Back home we ate loads of greens. The food was very healthy and you could see that by the build of the people, who had lots of muscle and no fat. I missed the greens, but I tell you what, when we found out about Chinese food, jeez! I can eat anything and everything and the Lucky Star on Holderness Road had it all. Our favourite was chicken chowmein, and it was fantastic. We would eat from there three or four times a week. But there was loads of choice. Back home pizza was something that only the rich people had seen in classy hotels, but here you could buy one in a cardboard box. Brilliant! But I had to rely on John to help me heat up my food. I didn't know how to use the microwave, the washer or the hoover and which one to put my pizza in so I just watched John, he knew what to do. This became a good excuse for me when I later met Jo and she suggested sharing the housework.

They would even let me have extra meals at the club during the week. There was a lovely couple there called John and Lynn and they really looked after me. After the game on a Sunday all the boys would come up as well and have gammon and chips. But I always got a massive mixed grill and the boys would say, 'hey what's going on here?' I was a bit shy so I just kept my head down but when I had got more confidence I said:

"When you sign your contract guys you need to make sure you get that extra clause in including your meals."

My reputation was starting to build and there were rumours that we would have to sell the team coach to pay for my food.

We had only been in England for about four weeks when Steve invited John and me round to his house for tea on Sunday. He said to come about five, so thinking we wouldn't have time for a meal later we headed off for the Lucky Star. Two chicken chowmeins, two fried rice, spare ribs, some prawn crackers and some more rice seemed to be enough. So we went home to eat our feast before we set off to Steve's for 'tea'. Surrounded by empty cartons we sat back in aching satisfaction, but now we had to get off our slightly fatter arses and round to Steve's.

As we walked up to Steve's house John said that he thought we might have overdone it a bit, and I was feeling stuffed as well. Hopefully Mrs Crooks wouldn't get any biscuits out but a nice cup of tea would wash it all down.

But when we walked into Steve's dining room, the horrifying realisation dawned on us. 'Tea' in Hull does not mean the colonial English cup of Earl Grey with a cucumber sandwich. It apparently means roast beef *and* roast pork, potatoes, vegetables and a huge Yorkshire pudding. Then it means, as a smiling Mrs Crooks announced:

"Treacle pudding with custard. There's extra for you two boys, Steve has told me how much you can eat. And there's more in the kitchen!"

Back home it is considered the height of rudeness to decline any food offered by a host. But it was ironic that the warmth and kindness of our new friends had given us our nearest death experience since we had arrived in the UK.

The kindness of the English, and their love of food and a night out became apparent very early in our first year over here. I was really excited when the boys at the club invited me and John to a 'gentlemen's' dinner'. This would surely be a posh occasion to have such a grand title. I guessed that they would be killing the best pig, or whatever the equivalent in the UK is, and everyone would be dressed in their finest clothes. John and I had learnt from our experience at Mrs Crooks' house and found out that there would be a three course meal at the dinner, and so we called the Lucky Star to let them know we wouldn't be round.

We all met at the club and then went in taxis to a social club on Hessle Road. But when we walked in it all felt a bit strange to me. It was quite dark and as I looked around I could see about a hundred men and just two women. Maybe the girls were at the wrong dinner, but they had certainly got dressed up for a special occasion. I was going to go and ask if they were lost but Steve said better not to and so we got some beers. Over the past few weeks we had already been to a couple of pubs with the boys, but I still couldn't believe that in England the beer was served in pints. I hadn't drunk that much when I was back home but when we went out in Hull we had pint after pint all night, and then got up in the morning to be sick. That's another great benefit of having a flushing loo, it's a must for the morning after! I wonder if the toilet companies had ever used that as an advertising idea –'Had a spew? Then flush the loo!' – pretty good eh?

We had the food which was about a quarter as good as Mrs C's and then settled down to listening to the speeches. I didn't really understand any of it, but it would be quiet for about ten minutes then everyone would laugh. Sometimes only one person would laugh so I thought the joke must be just for him. It seemed like this was going on forever and then the evening took a surprising twist.

One of the ladies that I'd seen at the beginning of the evening, got up onto the stage and stripped herself naked (I have never told Jo this story so hopefully she hasn't read this far, I'll know when she has). The other lady then came up and stripped off, and then they started doing this dance with a banana! I can't tell you what happened next but soon they were off the stage and sitting on guys' knees and kissing them. This was making me feel really uncomfortable and I just didn't know where to look.

Then things got dramatically worse. The two ladies, still with no clothes on started walking towards us. I looked at John and said:

"Mate, I think they're coming to get us. What can we do?"

We turned around and there were two big bouncers at the main door. In a wild panic we got up and just ran through the doors, we didn't open them we just crashed straight through, winging the bouncers as we went, and then we sprinted down the street. We could hear the boys running after us and shouting and eventually Steve caught us up and said:

"Hey lads don't worry it's just a show. Come on, come back in."

But we just jumped in a taxi and went home. What an experience. And for John and me, our education now had a sound base. We already knew what tea was and that when gentlemen have a special dinner you need to be prepared!

Other than food and beer, the other major expense for me was clothes. I had never seen so many clothes shops of all different types. Our wages weren't that high as Hull KR was still a part time club. We were paid £50 a week, but our rent and bills were covered as well, and we also got £300 win bonuses, so I tried to save some to take home to PNG at the end of the season. And clothes didn't cost too much. I didn't realise that the shops I was going into were charity shops. I thought it was a bit funny that the shop assistants were all old ladies but they had so much choice and didn't seem at all expensive. I'm sure I made a few fashion balls ups but haven't we all? And I bet yours cost you a lot more! I think that's all I need to tell you about my dress sense. Modelling isn't a career option when I retire!

◆

Learning about the way of life in my new country helped me to settle in at the club too. We were in National League Two and as we only trained three nights a week at the time, John and I had plenty of time for learning. We'd done meals out, dinners, driving and Chinese. So we spent most of our days asleep, in the shops or at the club. Well you have to start somewhere.

But soon the season was upon us and it was time to get down to business and show why we were here and what we could do. I couldn't wait for the first game, and I knew that the heartland of Rugby League was in the north of England and I'd heard of the famous names of Wigan, Leeds and Bradford. So we set off for South Wales – a completely different country! We drove and drove and drove and arrived there cold and exhausted. But the journey was worth it.

When we arrived we were met by two hundred travelling Rovers fans, the diehard supporters that are the lifeblood of any club, and would go to the end of the world to give us a lift. I swear I can still see nearly all of those two hundred now. Not just in my mind, but at Craven Park every home game and at away grounds all over the country. Those are the people who made my heart burst with pride when I went over the line at Hull F.C. last year. They've grown older, some of them have got married and have kids, and the older ones are even older. But they're still there, cheering when we win and devastated when we lose, whether at the Millennium Stadium or in Whitehaven. Every time I see them it puts a smile on my face especially now that they're back where they belong. Thanks to every one of you.

I had a dream start, scoring two tries and we won 70-8. The fans came up to me after to shake my hand, and I was so proud to be part of this team. This was a strong team with fire in its belly and full of good players, and we had great fans. I knew we didn't belong at this level even then. Don't get me wrong, the stadium in South Wales was better than I was used to but Hull KR shouldn't have been there. I had already heard stories of the Rovers team that dominated the game only fifteen years earlier. Some of the two hundred fans were too young to remember that, and I wondered if they would ever get the chance to see their team at the top level again.

There was one crazy fan I got to know called John. I started to wonder if everyone in Hull was called John. He's a taxi driver now but back in 1996 he was a bus driver and he used to do the run up and down Holderness Road. So whenever he saw me he'd toot his horn and I'd jump on and pass a bit of time with him, chatting to the passengers. John would go to hell and back for the club, in fact he probably has. And when I watch the telly or read newspapers and hear fans having a go at their club, particularly in football I think that fans like John have earned the right to do that. But it's usually the glory seekers who criticise, the real fans just want you to win.

Much as I loved riding around town on the bus I thought I'd better start to look for ways to fill my time, and so I came into the club every Monday to help John McLane to clean all the boots and sort the kit. I really enjoyed doing it because at home I got so bored, and at the time John had just had a hip replacement so he didn't mind me coming down.

 I was starting to feel like I really belonged here and I'm sure that made it easier for me on the pitch. Even though right through the season there were times when my team-mates couldn't understand what I was saying, which sometimes upset me, we went from strength to strength. And I was getting into my game and scoring tries which gave me more confidence. There was just one thing that I still couldn't cope with too well. The bloody weather!

At one game, I think it was in Barrow, in the first half it started snowing so I just ran back in, straight into the toilet to try to find a radiator! Everyone was looking for me on the field but

I'd disappeared. Eventually the physio came in to find me and said:

"Stan, what are you doing? You should be out on the field."

In a stirring moment of honesty I replied:
"I can't – it's too cold."

All the fans thought I had the shits, so I thought it better to leave it like that.

So I quickly found out that I couldn't do just what I wanted, and there was a lot of discipline in the game over here in England. Back home you could just get hold of the ball and run, and that's exactly what we did. But I had to learn to play the game on everybody else's terms, particularly the coach's! Steve kindly says that he never fell out with me, but I'm sorry to say that's not quite right.

I think his patience ran out at Whitehaven one afternoon. Come to think of it, it was the day after he had picked me and John up from the pub, so it would have been a good idea to follow his instructions. It's always physical up at Whitehaven, and they have big heavy players, so I figured I should run around them but after a first half pasting Steve tore a strip off me:

"And Stan, we might all be shit but what the hell can everyone else do when you're playing your own fuckin' game? For Christ's sake run like a forward and not a fuckin' Harlem Globetrotter! Otherwise the next time you leave your car in Beverley you're on your own!"

It probably wasn't the right time to ask what a Harlem Globetrotter was. But I'm sure that was the only time we had a fall out, and Steve let me get away with more than enough. It worked for me and it worked for the team. We all played hard and as the season went on we got stronger and stronger and we were soon beating teams for fun. I was really enjoying myself, playing my rugby and living my life. And I always enjoyed playing away, because everywhere we went was a brand new experience to me. I saw a new stadium every time, and back then they were all better than I was used to. All things are relative though.

I always reminded myself that back home in PNG we just got changed in the corner of the ground and, and in international matches, to ensure we had the best facilities we went to the nearest hotel to shower and change. But I give credit to the teams from Great Britain, France and Australia because they had to do that too, it was particularly funny watching the French guys looking for the personalised towels. So everything I saw over here was a wonder to me. We sometimes went to grounds and the boys were complaining saying, 'God the toilets stink' but I thought they were really nice!

But I have to say the most basic facilities you'd find in England were at Leigh. The visitors' dressing room wasn't big enough for the whole team to get in. Sometimes I think it's the psychology of the game though, when the away team gets the smallest room in the stadium and there's no hot water.

And in Salford there must be something in the water that stunts everybody's growth. The changing rooms were so low that it was okay for the smaller guys but the big boys had to get changed in the toilet. The dressing rooms were underneath one of the stands but obviously too near the pitch. I don't think they have won many architectural awards.

♦

Regardless of where we went and who we played against we were winning and I couldn't have been happier. I was scoring more tries as we went along and every week I sent pictures and cuttings home to my family back in New Guinea. I missed them all and I wanted them to see as much of what I was doing as possible.

I couldn't believe it when I was named 'Player of the Season' in League Two and I was the highest try scorer. Twelve months ago I was helping Mum pick coffee and dodging snakes. It was then that I really missed my family because I was having such a great time and I wanted them to share it with me. I'd got twenty-six tries in twenty-two starts and I was perfecting my somersault try that I'd been working on since I first played in Goroka. I loved doing it even when I could hear a grumpy Barrow fan shouting 'dickhead'! But the best thing of all was that we were promoted and to see the smiles on the faces of all our fans, especially the 'Magnificent Two Hundred' was a great reward.

Crooksy deserved it too. He's a fantastic guy and he is one of those people who I genuinely think have shaped my life and helped me to get to where I am. He was like something between a dad and a big brother to me when I first arrived, coming to get me when I got lost, bollocking me when I did wrong, and taking me to see a strip show. But I knew he was always looking out for me, which was a great comfort at a time when I had jumped in at the deep end.

Eventually the celebrations died down and everyone wound down for the close season and for me it meant the chance to go back to PNG to see my folks. It did all seem a long way away now but my heart was pounding at the thought of walking back into my village. But I wasn't going back until the beginning of October and so I had some time to kill. John was staying over until October too and so we started to think about what we could do to fill our time. No need. Steve was on the phone:

"Guys, I've got a job for you. We've got some work to do down at the ground."

'Some work' meant digging a new drainage system right around the perimeter of the pitch. To be fair Steve worked with us all the time, but for a whole week, John and I sweat buckets and swore by the minute as we dug a half-metre ditch right around the ground. That was after we had smashed through the surface concrete. This was certainly an abuse of the 'bob a job week' concept!

John and I had both lost nearly a stone and it was with some expectation that we wandered down to the ground during a day of British summer rain. Needless to say the new drainage system didn't work. I have no idea why. To this day I still wonder whether Steve had harboured a simmering grudge after we had tested his patience for a year.

♦

I was so excited to be going home. I had been ringing my Mum all year, but in September I was ringing every day and speaking to all my family telling them what I'd been doing, and that I was looking forward to seeing them all. It came as no surprise then that the phone bill was a little higher for the month than usual. Even John was shocked:

"Nine hundred and seventy eight pounds! Shit man, how are we going to get that through?"

It was a fair question. The club paid for all our bills. And we'd had plenty of win bonuses but nine hundred and seventy eight pounds! Shit. I had only saved one thousand pounds to take home; surely the club would cover this? After all they'd covered my food bill. As we had been a bit slow to learn the adage 'don't bite the hand that feeds you' this was, not altogether unexpectedly, the last phone bill they paid.

So this had been one hell of a year. In every single day I had learned something new. I longed to see my family and my village again but I wondered at all the things I had seen, all the people I had met, and all the experiences I had been through.

I was the English National League Two Player of the Year and I lived in a flat that had a flushing toilet.

Now that is something to be proud of.

4

Up, Up and Away

1997-1999
Hull Kingston Rovers

Going home to Papua New Guinea at the end of my first season in the UK was the most incredible experience. I had only been in England for seven months or so, but it seemed that I'd been away for much longer. And I just wanted to see my village again, see my mum, my brothers and my uncles, and eat some greens. On the flight home I felt kind of nervous as well as excited. I had so much to tell everyone, although I guess they already knew most of it, as my phone bills would testify. But how would everyone back home react when I arrived? Would they be anxious to see me? Would they come to the airport to meet me, after all I hadn't been away that long? I was sure that at least Mum would be there.

I thought I'd ring home when I landed at Port Moresby as the flight on from there to Goroka would only be an hour. When we began our descent over New Guinea, I looked out of the window and saw the great mountains and the deep green rainforest coming into view. I was nearly home. It was late September and so the weather would be …. hot. So I was beginning to regret wearing jeans, jumper and coat, although t-shirt and shorts would have looked just as badly planned in the departure lounge in Manchester, where it was cold and rainy.

As we landed at Port Moresby I couldn't believe my eyes. It was just amazing; I could see as soon as I stepped off the plane that the whole place had gone crazy. There were news reporters and television cameras everywhere, and the airport was packed with people waving, shouting and getting the best view to see me. Some officials from the PNG rugby league showed up as well, and then I began to realise again the magnitude of what I had done. Someone told me that I was only the second ever rugby league player from PNG to return home after playing a season in England. I was completely overwhelmed. I knew that rugby league is a religion in PNG, but this was beyond everything that I could have imagined. It was a wonderful experience to know that all these people had remembered me, and had been looking out for me. And I was now more excited than ever to be home.

If the greeting in Port Moresby took my breath away, arriving in my home town was something else again. As we flew towards the little airport at Goroka I could see the village and my house. Tears of happiness began to stream down my face. And when I stepped off the plane I got goose bumps because I could see the crowds of people that were here too, and I was so proud to be back. But the difference here was that this was my home town, and I would know a lot of the faces. The airport was full of local people, men, women, girls and boys had all heard that I was coming home from England. At times like this you know where you belong, and I had to pinch myself to check that I was really home.

The airport was packed but soon I could see my Mum and then I found it hard not to cry again. But it was one of the happiest moments of my life. I could see the look of relief on her face, and I'm sure there was the tiniest bit of pride there too. Mum was very unhappy when I had decided to go to England to play rugby at the beginning of the year. She had worked so hard to pay for me to go to school, and had high hopes that I would go on to train to be a teacher. She still wasn't happy with that, but when she saw how excited the local people were to see me she smiled the way only your mum can smile, and I knew, as I always did, that she was on my side.

It's funny because arriving home for the first time was an incredible experience, anybody and everybody was there. But I have to say that the following year it was still exciting, but not quite as busy. And as people got used to it and everybody got to know that I was coming home every year, there were less and less there to greet me. So much so that a few years ago even my Mum stopped coming, and when I got home she was sitting in the house! In fact, last year my mum saw my brother Ben wearing a new t-shirt one day and she said, 'hey when did Stanley get home?' I know she still loves me the same but I was glad I made the most of the first homecoming.

And the first time Maul and Kaula, my adoptive Mum and Dad, were there at the airport too. Maul was just crying, like she does every time I go home, and I had to say: 'Hey I'm not dead, I'm here, and I'm alive'. It always upsets Maul when I'm leaving and she cries again when she hears the plane taking off. I'm very lucky to have two mums. Kaula said that he had noticed a difference in me. He said that I was more confident and my skin had gone lighter. I promised him I wasn't about to get a pet monkey and start singing!

But paler or not I had left home as a PNG footy player and come back as an English League player. I was so proud to be home and when I think about it now it still gives me those goose bumps.

We walked the ten minutes up to our village surrounded by family and friends, and I knew that my return would mean one thing for sure. They had killed a pig. In New Guinea any special occasion is bad news for the pigs. It's sort of like the Christmas decorations going up if you're a turkey in Britain, but I guess that the pigs back home are cooler about it as it isn't just one big massacre at the same time every year. And I can't imagine all the pigs sucking their stomachs in when they heard I was on the way!

Life was like a dream for me now and I couldn't have been happier. While I was home I even played some footy for PNG. We had two tests against New Zealand and then a perfect fixture for me, against Great Britain at Lae. I can remember bursting with pride at the thought of playing for my national team against my new adopted country. I had a really good game and we put on a great show. We scored more tries than GB, which we knew we could, but they kicked more goals, and finally we lost by six points. The strangest part of all was that Phil Lowe, the GB team manager, came to see me after the game. He had brought my last pay cheque from Hull KR, which I hadn't picked up before I left. The difference between my two lives, in Hull and in New Guinea was as clear as ever. The PNG internationals weren't paid for playing, and they didn't expect to be. I remembered how I felt the first time I realised that Hull KR were going to pay me. These are two different worlds.

♦

I'll always look back to my first return home as being the most special, but I look forward to it every year. I usually stay for a couple of months. It's a great chance to recharge my batteries and I get back to England feeling like a new player. And so when I returned to Hull in January I was just as excited as the year before, but with the team now playing in National League One it was going to be even better.

I still couldn't read or speak very good English, so I was completely oblivious to some of the things that were happening at Hull KR when I returned. To me Rovers looked like a healthy and well run club, any team with hot showers has to have some money! But the financial situation was anything but healthy. I saw accountants walking about the place every day, but in all honesty I didn't think anything of it. I was just here to play footy and that was all I wanted to do. And in any case, you don't have to come from overseas to glaze over when someone talks about CVA's and administration. Give me a footy any day and leave the business to the guys who wear glasses.

But I did know that something was wrong. I went to a supporters meeting where they showed video clips of us getting promoted the season before. I later found out that they were talking about the Rovers merging with Hull F.C, and Hull KR as a club disappearing altogether. I could see the passion and anger in the eyes of the fans. And they vowed to fight for the club, come what may. I'm pretty sure Neil Hudgell and his mates were there, and I remember thinking back to the two hundred fans I had first encountered in South Wales. This club wouldn't just disappear. And I already understood enough about the rivalry in the city to know that I would never play for Hull F.C. There was more chance of Blue Peter fixing a kiddies' competition, and if that ever happened surely hell would freeze over!

All the senior players had to meet with David Thornhill, the chief accountant, to talk about this year's contracts. When it was my turn I was glad that I had taken Paul Fletcher's advice to use his agent, a nice bloke called Derek who certainly looked the part with his briefcase and pony tail. Surely this accountant, with his vast business experience and catalogue of qualifications, would be no match for Derek!

Partly through a lack of knowledge and language, but mainly through complete disinterest, I just let them get on with it. As they tapped into their calculators and showed each other the screens, I was thinking to myself that I had come to the UK with nothing, and so what was the big deal? Back home I lived off the land and here in England you could buy absolutely anything, and people shouted my name wherever I went. I didn't want any more money I just wanted to carry on playing for Hull KR. Derek had told me not to say that! A few times actually.

So after I had spent half an hour looking out of the window, and then comparing the sizes of their two briefcases, we all shook hands and we left. Derek had negotiated a 600 per cent increase for me, and I was now earning £12,000 a season plus win bonuses, that's a lot of chow mien. So I guessed that the club was clearly in good health.

The biggest thing I noticed playing in National League 1 was that the standard of rugby was much better. There were sides like Wakefield, Widnes and Halifax in the league and there were a lot of good players around.

But we had our own stars that were as strong as any in the league and I had already made some good friends on the pitch. No more so than Rob Wilson. People often misunderstood Rob and a lot of fans, especially not ours, thought he was a psycho. That was probably because he was always fighting. But he was brilliant for me and very early on he had said:

"Stan, if anyone gets you on the field I'll come after them mate. If you get stuck in I'll back you up."

It was like having a cross between Wyatt Earp and Hannibal Lector as your minder. If anyone did so much as push me, I'd look behind and Rob would be standing there with a mad look in his eyes, and you could hear the player shit his pants. It was kind of funny but I was always glad he was on my side.

The guy who had really made me feel welcome off the field was Paul Fletcher. He was the clown of the team, always kidding around on away trips, putting salt in the sugar bowl at the table and stuff like that. I thought that was brilliant and I didn't realise that people had done it before. He got me in trouble more than once, messing up my hotel room after I'd left. I'm sure that was because he liked me! Who needs enemies? But Paul was a big member of the team in every sense, the longest serving player and a very loyal friend. After all, without Paul I wouldn't have had an agent, a new car or very salty tea.

I loved every minute of the 1997 season and was playing the best footy of my life. You could see that the club was going places and we were playing in front of 4,000 fans some weeks, double what we were used to. We were still winning and I started to believe that one day I could play in the Super League with Rovers. We could certainly live with the teams at this level, and we made it to the Plate Final to prove our point. This was my first experience of a final in England and is one that I will never forget.

We played Hunslet at Wembley in the curtain raiser to the 1997 Challenge Cup final, between St Helens and Bradford. It was weird for me, because for the whole of the week before the boys had been talking about Wembley, but I didn't really know why they were so excited.

But by the Saturday morning I was as eager as anyone, and when we arrived at the ground I couldn't wait to look around. We walked out onto the Wembley pitch and I stared about me in absolute wonder. The stadium was nearly a hundred years old but to me it looked brand new. And it was massive. I just looked all around imagining what it would be like full of fans singing and cheering. Some had already started to arrive and I had my first real sense of the size of the occasion. This was a real opportunity for Rovers to make our name, and my first chance to play on a world class stage.

We were due to kick off at 12-30, and with ten minutes to go we were ready. Everyone was pumped up, shouting at each other and clenching their fists. And finally the time was here, this was the proudest moment of our careers, we were walking down the Wembley tunnel.

And then we were walking back up it. Shit! Some guy ushered us around, and back to the changing rooms, because there had been a bomb scare. The boys couldn't believe it and Rob was pacing up and down like a crazed tiger. I couldn't help pitying the first guy who tackled him today. Our big moment had arrived and some tosser had left his butty box on the athletics track!

So I lay down on the physio's table, determined to stay calm and focussed. Actually I didn't have any problem staying calm … in fact I fell asleep. I don't know for how long. But the next thing I remember was staring up at the white ceiling, with Andy Danatt's face looming into view. Everyone else was back in the tunnel and Andy, the last one out had heard me snoring from around the corner. If I wasn't such a noisy sleeper, they could have gone out onto the pitch without me! I splashed water over my face and ran out.

Lucky for me that Andy woke me up. We played a blinder, winning 60-14, and more than anything this was a reward for our brilliant supporters who'd come down to London in their thousands. I remember that with about twenty minutes to go the ground was filling up. Our fans were mixing with the lads from Bradford and St Helens and the atmosphere was electric. Wembley held over 75,000 people and I had never seen such a crowd before. I scored a hat trick and won the 'man of the match' and only after the game did Andy tell the boys how he had found me asleep five minutes before kick-off.

After the final whistle they set up a presentation stand on the pitch and we received the trophy. I can remember getting a little box with a medal and a cheque for £1,000 for winning the 'man of the match'. Some of the boys were grabbing bits of the turf, and stuffing them into their socks, to take home as a souvenir. And someone told me I had scored the first hat trick ever in a Wembley final, and I just couldn't wait to ring home to tell my mum. Thank God I rang her before I got on the bus, because three hours later I could hardly speak. I had never drunk so much beer in my life. There was so much booze on the bus and we never got past sixty all the way home. But as Crooksy always told me, 'when in Rome do as the Romans do'. I still have the suit I wore that day but it looks pretty terrible. I never had it cleaned, because at the time I didn't know about dry cleaners, and all I could think of was to put it through the washing machine.

♦

The Wembley final was one of the two life changing events that I had in 1997. By the middle of the footy season I felt ready to put down some roots. I thought that I had already learned a lot about life in England, and I seemed to be able to get on with the people here. Maybe it was time to settle down and get a girlfriend.

I was in Prince's Quay shopping centre when I first saw Jo, a really pretty, tiny, blond girl. I'd seen the adverts on television where a bloke runs up to a girl he doesn't know, and gives her a bunch of flowers. I think it was for hairspray. But obviously in real life that's all bollocks, and I was just pleased that I managed to pluck up the courage to say hello to her. You have to understand that for me it was very scary. Scary in that I was trying to make a friendship with a white girl. I never dreamed in a million years that I could be with a white girl; it just seemed too wild to be true. I don't know how to explain it properly. It would be easy to have a girlfriend back home in New Guinea that I could talk to in my own language. But here I had to think about what I was saying all the time. It was so scary, but I'm glad I found the courage to ask her out. It was God given. Everything about Jo was perfect. The way she looked, the way she was. I knew right away that she was warm and kind and she was so easy to be with. I couldn't believe that I'd found a girl like this. It was like one out of a thousand. And I couldn't believe it when she asked if I wanted to go out with her on her sister's birthday the week after.

I went along and had a great time, we just clicked straight away and I wanted to see Jo again as soon as possible.

So we went to the pub for our second date, it seemed the right thing to do. Back home I had never been in a relationship, but I knew from watching the boys that over here, the pub is the way to charm a girl. Jo had her own car and she came to pick me up. She was dressed up and looked beautiful, and I couldn't believe she was trying to impress me. But she had a lot to live up to because I was wearing my green Levi jeans and cream polo shirt that I'd just bought from the charity shop. I knew I looked cool! And I was determined to make the most of my chance.

Two pints of John Smiths and a packet of crisps; I really know how to treat a girl. Jo reminds me about our first date now, and laughs at my terrible choice of venue, but it looks like I got away with it.

Looking back I don't know how Jo coped with me. As time went on she had to put up with more and more. In summer during the night I still used to take my mattress off the bed and put it down by the radiator, and poor Jo was boiling.

And she is a vegetarian, but I didn't give a donkey's. I had never lived with a vegetarian before; I would eat my mixed grills right in front of her and sometimes I'd take her to KFC. But somehow, thank God, she could see something in me and we just seemed to click. We carried on seeing each other and had a great time. We always had a laugh and I felt more relaxed the longer we were together. And it wasn't long before she took me round to see her mum and dad.

But this worried me more than anything. And I started to think, 'this just isn't right.' I tried to compare Jo's family and mine, and in my own
mind they just didn't meet. I was constantly asking myself if it was all real. Why was Jo attracted to me? It just didn't make any

sense to me at all. When we arrived at their house I became even more scared. It was beautiful and looked just like a show house.

Up to this point Jo hadn't really known that I was a rugby player. I had been lying to her, telling her that I was a university student, studying P.E. She said to me one day that she had seen in the papers someone who looked like me on the sports pages. So to keep the lie rolling I said, 'It must be my brother, he's a rugby player and he looks just like me.'

She had already told her mum and dad that her boyfriend was black. And knowing them as I do now, it is no longer a surprise that they just told her to bring me along. What I hadn't counted on was that Jo's dad, Paul, was a Hull KR fan when he was younger and kept a keen eye on the Rovers. So when Jo introduced me as Stanley he looked right in the eyes, then his eyebrows went up and he said:

"Oh hi Stanley, come in, it's nice to meet you Stan. You're doing well at Rovers. Jo didn't tell me you were a rugby player!"

Actually, as it turned out Jo had known for some weeks, and I'm sure she'd told her dad as well. I think she was just waiting for me to come clean:

"I knew you were lying you daft sod. I kept seeing the pictures in the paper and they were the spitting image of you. And I've never even met your brother!"

I guess it was a stupid plan but it seemed like a good idea at the time. I didn't want Jo to stay with me just because I was a rugby player. But I had underestimated her already.

As the relationship started getting a bit more serious I kept asking myself if it was all real. But I stopped trying to compare Jo's family and their beautiful clean house with my folks back home. I realised that there was nothing to compare and that they were both as important as each other in their own way. And one night it all came out of me. I arrived home smashed and blurted out:

"If you really like me and you really want to see where I'm from, then why don't you come home with me?"

So she did. And even more amazingly, she came back again and again. It can't have been that Jo liked hanging around in airports waiting for me, or even had a new founded fascination with spiders. But I honestly think she was blown away by the warmth and welcome of my people and my family. And of course this is something that Jo knows all about. But in Hull, a welcome might be a handshake and a beer, or being invited round for 'tea', all of which is great to be offered. But in PNG a warm welcome is rather different.

Jo admitted that when she first went to PNG she was frightened, and so was her family. It can't have helped when I missed her incoming flight, but when we landed at Goroka my whole family was there to meet her. The people from my village had turned up in their traditional tribal dress and did a war dance for her. For a lot of people, having been stranded in an airport in a strange land for two hours, this might have been all too much. But Jo recognised the importance to my people, and the warmth of the reception, and she was overwhelmed.

They put a garland of flowers around her neck and as we walked to the village they threw flowers on the path in front of her. It was very moving for Jo and she loved the way she had been welcomed with open arms. At that point of course, she didn't know that I'd invited a tree full of spiders into my house. But come to think of it, I guess the way my family and friends immediately loved Jo probably did me a huge favour!

She had celebrity status from the moment she arrived. It was difficult for a lot of the people there to understand how I had returned home with a white girl on my arm. But it was true, and now that I was with Jo on my home ground, I could really believe that this was my girl for sure.

Every time we walked to the market, Jo would turn round to see a group of little kids following us. And the way she smiled at them made them follow even more. The old people in the market were a bit more forward. Jo had long blond hair and so the old women would pull it just to see if it was real or not.

And the first time she came, she stayed out in PNG for a whole month, which I knew was very brave of her. To come so far on her own, to a culture about as removed from the UK as possible, needs a strong mind and a big heart. Not to mention coming to a land full of giant creepy crawlies, and to cap it all as a vegetarian. Even the pigs were pleased to see Jo when she arrived!

We had planted loads of sweet potatoes for her, to go with the greens, and most of the time she did alright. But whenever she struggled for food I took her to the hotel in Goroka. My mum told me that I should take Jo to live in the hotel because I had enough money to do that. But Jo was hearing nothing of it. She had come to my home to see my family and live as we do. And that told my mum as much about my girlfriend as she needed to know.

♦

So Jo had survived her first visit to PNG, and I had survived my first two seasons in Hull. If it hadn't all been plain sailing so far, it had certainly been fun. And as I was getting a lighter shade every season, I would blend in completely in thirty years time, so long as no one asked me for a lift. And I didn't wet myself every time it snowed now. But behind the scenes things were happening that could have changed Jo's and my lives dramatically.

I was told, months later, that after the 1997 Plate Final, Rovers had received an approach from St Helens, and they had reputedly offered £60,000 to take me to the world centre of glass, and the home of Johnny Vegas. Who knows what might have happened, and most importantly, how easy it would be for Jo to move so far from her home. In many ways to go from Hull to Merseyside for Jo, was as much of an upheaval as travelling around the world was for me. When you are so close to your own family, a hundred miles can sometimes seem like ten thousand.

I think I'm glad that I didn't find out. And that Rovers showed the ambition to turn down a really big cash offer. It must have been tempting for the accountants to collect the money on offer, and I guess it showed that they were taking a

A proud dad, with Leo and Elliott

My first house - I thought it was luxury

Kaula and Maul - I owe them everything

I was always happy at Huddersfield

Don't try this at home

Baby Stan and Christina

long term view and had the interests of the club at heart. I would have found it very hard at that stage in my life to leave my 'home town' team. And so, blissfully unaware, I turned up for duty again in 1998.

I honestly thought that this would be the year for us. I was starting to get a burning feeling inside me that made me want to play at the highest level I could - in the Super League. And I knew that this Hull KR team could get there. Things were going well at the club and we were really gathering some speed. We had gone from promotion in 1996, to winning the Plate Final the following year and for me there was a feeling of real excitement about the place.

The supporters were as loyal as ever, and I remember that they worked so hard at fund raising for the club, and they actually collected enough money to bring over two young Australian players. The club was so lucky to have supporters like these, who would go to the end of the earth to help. And the players owed it to the fans to work as hard as we could to bring more success.

I felt that I was playing better all the time. For one thing I was getting used to being coached properly. But I also understood the language more easily, and I was learning to speak it as well so that I could work well with the team. It didn't come easily to me; it was my fourth language and the hardest that I'd learnt.

And I was starting to get used to the cold!

I ran my heart out all year, took plenty of shots and handed a few out, and I eventually ended up with thirty four tries from thirty six appearances. The one game that really sticks in my mind was the derby at Boothferry Park. Simply because it was against our fierce rivals Hull F.C. They had a very strong team, and for as long as I had been in Hull they had always been ahead of us. This was my first experience of a derby, and I soon knew exactly what it meant to our fantastic supporters for us to beat Hull. Like any underdogs, you are battered by taunts and have to endure endless cocky boasts, and this leaves a scar. You can see in these games that in the faces of our fans, there aren't just the normal expressions of joy and despair, but also an intense pressure, as if this was more than just a game. But a game it was. And we bloody won it!

I felt like a wild animal tasting blood for the first time. Once you've tasted it, you just want it again and again. Hull KR was now well and truly in my veins, and wherever my playing career took me, I would always support the Rovers, no matter where I was.

We were strong throughout the season, beating the favourites, Wakefield, twice by very big margins. So we would surely have a great chance of beating them again when we met in the play offs. But something happened to us. I can't explain it properly but we never actually looked like winning the game. Then we had a second chance to play them again, and we lost again.

Why did we play so poorly when it came to the crunch? I was gutted. And frustrated like hell. I really thought that we were going to the Super League, and then my hopes just fizzled out. And I felt sorry for the supporters who had given everything they had. But we would live to fight again, next time with even more ferocity.

♦

It was during the 1998 season that I came across one of the biggest, funniest, most outrageous characters in the game. He was an imposing guy, with a sharp wit and a mischievous smile always lighting up his bright, red face. He could give the most uplifting speeches without preparation, and could raise your spirits when you were at your lowest ebb.

The first time I met the great John Leeman he was swearing. I can't remember why he was swearing, but it struck me that it was weird for a man wearing a pastor's outfit to be talking like a second row. I thought that he must be on his way to a fancy dress party. There is a big difference between dressing up back home, and over here in England. In PNG to make a tribal costume we take the best feathers from the birds of paradise, scoop out their bodies, and then they are carefully entwined and positioned by an expert, to make the spectacular headdress. It takes hours to dress this way, but is a tradition passed down for thousands of years.

In the UK, for fancy dress, you just wear your wife's underwear or go to a shop to hire a chicken suit; a tradition which I'm sure has been passed down for centuries as well! But this was no fancy dress. The *Reverend* John Leeman was the club chaplain ..... he was a man of the Church.

And he was such a funny guy. He even used to swear when he said grace as we all sat round for our pre match meal! He was nothing like the swearing priest on 'Father Ted'; he was as sharp as a knife and always held everyone's attention. He was very much like Paul Fletcher in the way that he could make people feel at home, just by the way he joked with them. And he constantly took the piss out of me, whenever he saw me getting excited by my growing fame in the town.

One day we were walking down Preston Road and I waved at a group of boys across the road. The Rev looked to the heavens and then at me, and I knew a divine intervention was on its way. He said:

"You know what Stanley. When you die, they'll have to bury you upside down with your feet sticking up in the air."

"Why's that John?"

"So that the whole damn world can kiss your big black arse!"

Amen.

But John had a heart as big as any I had seen. He was the also the headmaster at Cogan School in Hull and when we visited we could see that the kids all loved him. He knew exactly how to look after people, and took a lot of time arranging trips and events for us. It was like having a guardian angel with a mild form of Tourette's Syndrome.

One Friday the Reverend took me, John McLane and two of the boys to London for a sightseeing trip. I had been to Wembley the year before, but we had arrived on the bus at the ground before the game, and got straight back on again after. So I had never seen the capital city before, and I didn't know what to expect.

We drove down to Rayner's Lane tube station in the morning, which took about four hours and gave me the chance to learn a few new words from the Reverend. And then we caught a tube train into the city centre. When we stepped off the tube I just couldn't believe it. It was just so, so busy. Everyone was pushing and walking really fast, and I remember it being very hot as well. Now I realised that in London they get warmer weather than in Hull.

But it turned out to be a really good trip. Firstly we went to see Buckingham Palace which was a big thrill for me. I saw the guards that you only see in the movies back home. It was great to see them in their traditional dress with their red uniforms and big black hairy hats, rather than wearing a chicken suit or vicar's outfit like I guess they did if they weren't on duty!

We went to see the Houses of Parliament. And then on the way to Tower Bridge we had to cross a very busy road. I was carrying my bags of souvenirs, and as I fumbled around I dropped my sunglasses in the middle of the road. We got to the other side and I was gutted that I had dropped them so I decided to get them back. I was very fond of my shades; they were Ray Bans that someone had given to me, so I dropped my bags and darted back into the road. Well you should have seen the fuss! I'm telling you it was way over the top. After all, I had put my hand up to stop all the cars, but I guess I had underestimated the volume of the traffic. The horns honking and people screaming at me were not unfamiliar to me, given my driving experiences in Hull, but the sheer number of aggressive drivers was. By the time the first car door opened we had made our speedy exit. And as we walked down Pall Mall we could still hear the horns beeping and could see that the traffic jam had grown quite a lot.

I don't know how, but when we got home the next day, the story of how I stopped the traffic outside the Houses of Parliament had hit the Hull Daily Mail. And at the next home game, every time I looked up, all the fans were waving their sunglasses at me. If I didn't know better, I'd think that the Reverend had had a quiet word!

Reverend John and the supporters groups always made me feel so lucky and grateful because they often arranged trips for us. It meant a lot to me that my new friends were looking after me in this way. One day they took me on a trip to York. And the best part for me was when we went to the Viking Museum. It was a real eye opener.

We went on a train which took us to this small mock up village. And one of the boys explained to me that this was exactly how people lived fourteen hundred years ago, when the Vikings came across the sea to England. In the village there were three or four small huts with a fence running around the back. You could see pigs and chickens running around and a woman cooking something in a hole in the ground.

There was this guy, wearing a big rough skin coat, sharpening a blade. And then there was the smell. Everyone winced as the guide explained that there was no sanitary system and people just used to shit in a hole in the ground. This was all fourteen hundred years ago. And then it struck me. Jeez, it just looked like home. This is how we live back in the rainforest now, and all of a sudden I felt, at the same time, self conscious, and a bit homesick. I remember thinking that it must be the first time that the Viking display had made a tourist dream of home.

♦

The 1999 season went the same way as the previous one. We were winning, but not getting to the top of the table and I was getting more and more frustrated. We were all putting our bodies on the line week after week, but it seemed that we were always destined to fall short. I loved playing at Craven Park, and I loved the supporters most of all, they had become like a family to me.

It's often in family situations that you can get the most emotional and intense. I started to think about the offer that St Helens had made for me two years earlier, and I have to admit that for the first time in my career at Hull KR I was feeling unsettled.

It didn't help that my coach and mentor Steve Crooks had already left. Crooksy had gone across the city to Hull. Why the hell had he done that? I couldn't understand it and I hadn't really talked to Steve about it. I didn't know what the ins and outs of the move were. But I did know that the man who had invited me for tea when I had first arrived in Hull, who had picked me up in town whenever I was lost, and was always looking out for me, had gone. Steve meant so much to me. The best way I can explain it is if he came to my village in PNG we would kill FIVE pigs for him. That's a measure of my thanks to Steve. So the same pigs that welcome Jo with open trotters would run like shit if they ever saw Steve's Volvo homing into view.

So like anyone who's seen their big brother leave the family, I started to wonder what it would be like. I had done it before, leaving my mum and brothers back home in New Guinea. But this was different again. There were already rumours that I might go to Hull. But I quashed these by saying in broken English that I'd rather cut off my dick with a rusty saw, although I don't think that was how it was printed in the Hull Daily Mail.

Jo knew that I was getting restless. And the important thing was that by this time we had become inseparable. We had a son, little Elliott, who was nearly two, and so we agreed that if we were going to do anything, we were going to do it together. And I trust Jo more than anyone in the world to tell me if I'm going to make the wrong decision. So that gave me the comfort that I wasn't going to be on my own.

I couldn't come to terms with the way Rovers had done so well in the past two years, but then fallen away at the end of each season after all the hard work. I started to wonder if it was ever going to happen for us. And the more I thought about it, and the more I spoke to Jo, I knew in my heart that I had made up my mind.

Derek and his ponytail had been busy, and he soon presented me with the chance that I was desperate for. To play in the

Super League, with a new team that was being put together in Gateshead. Thank God it wasn't Hull. And it wasn't all that far away either. But even though we had agreed to take the chance, Jo and I were both frightened by the thought when it became reality. Surely we were doing the right thing. We had come to know each other so well, and since I had settled down, I had stopped living life from day to day. I had more responsibilities now and I had to plan for the future. This would be the next step. And I had never regretted my first big gamble; to come to Hull in the first place.

It became common knowledge around the club that I was going, and when the last game of the season came, I was more than a little nervous. I was probably even more nervous because I wasn't playing, I was injured. And I wondered what it would be like watching the lads play, as a team mate, for the last time.

I sat in the stands at Featherstone, watched us lose, and then stood up to make my way out. I felt a bit disappointed to be leaving the club I loved in this way. But before I had the chance to move I was astounded by what happened next. I shouldn't have been, because I knew what a special bunch of people the Hull KR fans are. A couple of hundred of them had run onto the pitch, I thought to mob the lads. But they made their way over to the stand where I was and started chanting my name and singing 'cheer up Stanley Gene'. Next thing, they had dragged me out of the stand and were carrying me shoulder high around the pitch, throwing scarves and banners at me. This was their reaction after they had just lost! For fans to lose a game and then still have the heart to celebrate with me made me feel very humble. I knew that they were wishing me well and my fears that there would be any bad feeling had disappeared.

But when they did this, it also made me feel very sad in a way. It suddenly hit me. This was the club that had, without question, changed my life beyond my wildest dreams. This was the club that had given me my chance in the UK. I had so many memories and made so many friends. I was going to leave home for the second time in my life. And this time wasn't any easier than the first.

But it was the right time. And if I didn't go now, I would spend the rest of my life wondering what would have happened to me next …..

5

Stan Gene's Schooldays

1979 - 1985
Goroka

Naked mud wrestling was popular with the kids in Segu, my village, long before the programme planners at Sky saw its potential as a spectator sport. It seems strange to me now, but when I was a little boy we all ran around our village with no clothes on. In a way it was a good thing, because we didn't have water in the village. The nearest creek was a ten minute walk away, and so washing clothes wasn't the simple routine that it is for us over here in England.

When we went to the market town or the city, of course we wore clothes; the people of PNG have their own high standards and codes of modesty, and nudity is not the thing. But back in the village we could spend our lives completely in the buff, and frequently in the mud. Up to the age of around six it's still the same now, and when I visit home it makes me feel sort of awkward. I think I must have been sanitised somehow during my twelve years in the UK. When I see a kid sitting in a puddle I have to stop myself from saying, 'hey, get out of there and put some clothes on'.

And not only were we completely at ease in the nude, we were very clever when it came to keeping ourselves amused. I was amazed when I first saw a park in England, with all sorts of things for kids to play on - swings, slides and climbing frames. The bush was our playground and we always found things to do. We could make swings on the trees, and mud sliding was a favourite game after a downpour.

It seems incredible now, but at the ages of four and five we even tried to build our own swimming pools! If it got really hot we'd go down to the creek and dig a big hole next to it that would soon fill with muddy water. But it was so cool that it was a great place to splash about in.

What would parents in England do if they found their kids sitting in a two foot deep mud bath? After putting the kid on a course of malaria tablets and typhoid injections, the puddle would be roped off by the council's health and safety department, whilst fighting off a claim issued by 'Mud Induced Illness Lawyers for You'. It wasn't really seen to be that big a risk in PNG.

I'm not saying that Maul and Kaula, or everyone else's parents, were carefree mums and dads. It just wasn't realistic to protect the children from danger all the time. Not with a billion snakes terrorising the country in any case!

I came to understand the meaning of danger pretty early on. And learning by experience is always the best way, particularly at a young age. Every hut had a fire in the middle of the room. We had no electricity or gas and so fire was the only source of light at night, and the only way to cook. And crawling about at the age of two or three, there was nothing to stop a kid touching the fire. That is the way you learn to associate the flames not only with warmth and colour, but also with terrible pain. And gaining that respect for fire at an early age makes sure that it is never something that you want to play with in later life.

◆

There was a lot of excitement and a big change for us in the village early in 1980. Everyone was saying there was going to be a new school. To be honest, we didn't actually know what a school was. But when the East Goroka Community School opened we all went along to find out, and it soon became a fantastic part of all our lives. Our days of running around just playing until nightfall were over. Now we had a school to go to, and this was a cause for real celebration. It was a chance for all of us to make as much of our lives as we could, and we accepted it with open arms.

Not that we no longer had any time to play. In the first grade the classroom was outdoors and we had our lessons under a tree. It takes good concentration to learn your 'A B C' while keeping an eye out for tree snakes! And because of this, when it rained the teacher sent us all home. But we always walked to school in the morning even when it was raining, just to be sent home again, because that was not our, or our parents decision to make.

And school was certainly good fun, even if I wasn't always sure exactly what was going on. My earliest memory of a lesson is sitting under the trees and singing:

"Aeroplane, aeroplane up in the sky,
Why are you going so fast and so high?"

We had absolutely no idea what we were singing because all the words were in English. We had been learning to say, 'hello, good morning' and a few other things. But it was many years later, when I had learnt more English and could put two or three words together, that it dawned on me what we had been singing. I was looking up into the sky at the time when an aeroplane flew past. It's great when something finally clicks.

The schooldays started early in the morning and ended soon after lunch, when the day was at its hottest. Then we walked home, collecting stones on the way, to use in our afternoon pursuits.

We spent every afternoon going into the bush with our sling shots and bags of stones, to go hunting for birds and bats, and looking for wild fruit. I can't remember anyone telling us that this is what we should do, there was never any question. It was just our way of life. We would spend hours in there. And I loved to collect firewood. So when we went home for tea, we always had armfuls of wood with us to take around the village, particularly to the old people. All the grown ups were pleased with us because we were already showing responsibility and care for our village. Firewood was the only fuel, the only way of keeping warm, of heating water and of cooking. Actually we didn't know that we were helping, collecting wood was our hobby. But just as in any close community, seeing people happy with you makes you want to help more. And we were learning at an early age that everyone in the settlement must do their bit, to help us all survive.

◆

Soon after the school opened, there was more activity in the village to excite the young kids. Every Sunday there was a cross country race, and it was organised by 'experts'. We called anyone who had white skin 'experts'. I think these were volunteers from the big high school in Goroka. They always showed up with huge sacks full of shredded paper. And when they set off to mark the course, they left trails of paper as they went. This really confused us because we didn't understand what they were doing.

I realise now that they left the trails because, coming from the city, they didn't know the jungle as well as we did. And so if they got lost, they would just follow the paper back to the village. But we never knew why they did that and it was always a source of great entertainment.

One Sunday morning, when our parents had gone to church, I was playing marbles with my two cousins, Wabe and Kobsy, in the nude of course. You should try it some day; you never know it might catch on! Then, at about ten o'clock we saw the experts had arrived, and they were starting to set a course. As they headed off into the bush they were shouting to us, 'on, on, on, on' and so the three of us ran after them full of excitement. They went right into the middle of the jungle on a long, winding route, and soon we had been running for well over an hour. We must have easily run ten miles. Eventually we got through the jungle and came out at the other end, and to our surprise we were at the back of the airport in Goroka.

Around the front of the airport is a small town, but it was very busy that morning. There was a market open and people were coming out of the church dressed in their Sunday clothes. Everyone dressed in their best clothes to go to church. It's weird, over here people get dressed up to go out to a nightclub.

But at home, you'd see people who didn't have nice clothes to wear, come Sunday would bring out a really good suit, and then put it back until the next Sunday. So at that very moment the street was filled with smartly dressed people; and then suddenly we remembered. All three of us looked downwards and discovered to our horror that we were naked. In all the excitement we had forgotten this important detail, and now found ourselves displaying our prized, if undeveloped, assets to the good churchgoers of Goroka!

Amid shouts of 'heavens above' and 'lord save us' we scuttled off to save our embarrassment. We ran through the airport leaving a trail of gasps, squeals and laughter, as the morning flight to Port Moresby was about to board. So the airport was full as well. Luckily we found a rubbish bin that was full of plastic bags. We tipped out the contents, and with the two handles on each side and a hole in the bottom, the carriers made a stylish pair of pants, if a little smelly. Thank God the walk back to the village was only ten minutes. But it wasn't easy holding on to our makeshift trousers as we walked.

So I had learned a valuable lesson. Always check that you aren't naked when you are chasing experts into the bush. Not a phrase you'll often hear in Hull, but useful nevertheless.

♦

I am always really grateful to my family for the way they brought me up and paid for me to go to school. My mum and dad worked so hard to make sure we had what we needed. We were never struggling, we had food and land. And we could bring money in selling coffee at the market. We were a subsistence family, and knew how to live off the land. From an early age I always used to go outside to get my own breakfast, from whatever I could find growing, maybe a pineapple or some wild fruits.

But we also had some money coming in to buy oil, rice, salt and sugar. As well as my mum Maul selling coffee and vegetables at the market, my dad Kaula worked as a labourer in the hospital at Goroka. I always felt sorry for my dad, because he worked his guts out. In the mornings and at the weekends he was working on the land. And during the day he went to the hospital. He never seemed to have any time to sit down and rest. My auntie, Christina, also worked in the hospital, and she gave Mum and Dad the money for my schooling. My school cost about a hundred Kina a year, which is about twenty quid, when I started. I didn't know why she gave so much at the time, but I did know that you could always get help from family. And Christina was always the first to offer help.

I learnt to love all kinds of food from as early as I can remember. My favourite supper of all was like a little worm that you find in the trees. You could find them in the trunk of the tree, or in the middle, where the biggest branches spread out. The worms lived in the tree wherever you could see sawdust. I've seen them on the telly, on documentaries where the SAS guy breaks them open to find the white worm and then he eats it to survive for three weeks. I've also seen them on 'I'm A Celebrity Get Me Out Of Here'. I think they call them wychety grubs on there. They make the 'celebrities' eat them to get the viewing figures up I'm sure. But to me it's really funny. It's a bit like if you saw me pulling a face like Paul Burrell crunching a kangaroo's bollock, whilst I was eating a fish finger. You'd think I was soft in the head.

I absolutely love them. And I can remember pestering Kaula to take me worm catching, the minute he walked through the door. My heart goes out to him, because I now realise that he was completely knackered after a long days work. He just wanted to relax, but I was crying at him, 'come on Dad let's go'. I wanted to go and hunt for worms every night. So, God bless him, he'd pick up his axe and we'd go off into the bush to look for the sawdust on the trees. Then he'd chop at the tree to get the skin off and I could pick up ten or twenty to take home for supper.

From the age of about six I knew how to cook the worms and they were delicious. They can be quite nice raw, but cooked they are a real delicacy. You can fry them in oil. But the way I really love them is to wrap them up in a cabbage leaf, with a bit of salt and just put them by the fire. You know they're ready when the cabbage starts to change colour and the worms are dead. It's a ready made meal, you can eat the cabbage with the worms and the taste is absolutely beautiful. Nowadays I put garlic in as well, very sophisticated. I've looked everywhere in Tesco's and East Park but you can't get them over here. That is, apart from at the ITV studios on the jungle set. And in any case, I think taking an axe into the park at nightfall might be frowned upon by the health and safety experts at the council!

This was without doubt my favourite food and I am grateful to Kaula, who never once refused to take me into the bush to find them, no matter how tired he was. I didn't realise at the time, but it hits me now that I am older. He was there for me every day, not just at the weekends, and I felt bad that I was always pestering him to take me out into the bush. We'd been doing it for years. Every year we had to go further and further into the jungle to find the worms because it took time for the trees to recover after we'd stripped them. God knows how many worms I must have eaten!

Before he passed away I said sorry to him, and he admitted then that he'd found it hard. When you're a kid you just think that your dad is there for you and you alone. But it's only when you are getting older, and you have kids yourself, that you truly see everything that your dad has done for you.

He was always there to play with me, to take me out into the bush and to teach me all he knew about the rainforest. He taught me to respect our country, all of nature and the value of working hard. I used to watch him, sitting there for hours making things. Carving an axe handle or sharpening a bush knife. It was the time taken to craft each item that made them perfect for the job. I learnt that tools were not for playing with; they were for working the land. They helped us to make money to buy food.

He felt passionately that we should respect the rainforest. And like all the guys of his generation, who used to carve at trees slowly and selectively, he hated the arrival of guys with chainsaws. All he could see when he heard the noise of a chainsaw was the birds and the wild animals being chased away. And he was right. He was a great dad and I miss him.

♦

We used to cook kau kau, the sweet potato as you know it, with almost every meal. Actually about ninety per cent of what we ate was vegetables. We were lucky that we had our own pigs, and so about every two weeks or so, or on special occasions we'd kill a pig. We ate the whole of the pig. Even the intestines and the tongue were really good, fried in a bit of oil. And when it was time to pick the coffee from our plantation, we would cook for anyone from the village who came to help us that day.

You'll know by now that killing a pig always signifies that something special has happened, or is about to happen. It was always a big occasion. And now and then it was really funny, because sometimes you'd see a guy wandering about the village muttering to himself, and to anyone near, 'I'm going to kill a pig … I'm going to kill a pig.'

The obvious tension was not always because there was a big event coming up. But more often it was actually that killing a pig wasn't all that easy. The tool designed to do the job was a kind of baseball bat made from the strongest branches of a coffee tree. And the method was to whack the pig, clean between the eyes. But you only had one chance. The pig, which'd already seen his mates disappear one by one, was always completely focussed on the guy with the bat. And if he missed, then the pig would launch a vicious attack. I've seen a few guys badly beaten up by a pig, only then to get a tongue lashing from all the family who had planned the feast back home!

Nowadays we shoot them.

♦

But from one day to the next it would always be kau kau, with greens and sometimes with rice. That made it a real treat. The rice with it made a really nice stew just cooked with a little bit of salt and oil. Sometimes we had tuna fish to put in, but the best ingredient to make the food really delicious was coconut and the coconut milk. I think that may be why many people in PNG are so strong and fit. The diet was pretty much ideal for athletes. So here in England I have to train very hard to keep my fitness. Without kebabs, burgers and pizzas on every corner it would be dead easy!

Back home, rice is very easy to get hold of now, but twenty-odd years ago it was expensive, and so it was even a special thing to be able to eat a bowl of rice just with oil and salt.

The first chance I had to see food from outside the village was when I went to the high school in Goroka about five years later. There were lots of kids from the city there, and it soon became obvious that there was one big difference between them and us - the packed lunches. My lunch was always a baked sweet potato, two or three sticks of sugar cane and sometimes a pineapple. Try eating that without a knife! But these guys were turning up with ham and corned beef sandwiches. At lunchtime we used to sit in a circle and look at what each other had. The city boys got fed up with their lunches and so we sometimes swapped our sugar cane for a sandwich. What a deal! I can remember eating a corned beef sandwich like a bar of chocolate. Just eating a bit at a time and waiting for it to melt in my mouth. We would have taken them home to show the little kids in the village, but it was far too hot and they would have melted. And they tasted so good.

♦

Back when the primary school opened in our settlement, we were the pioneers. Because there hadn't been a school there before, we formed a first grade. There were three classes of about twenty kids in each. The following year, we became the second grade and the next lot of kids came in to first grade, and so on, and that's how the school was formed. Before the school opened, kids either went to school in Goroka, or more often not at all.

In the first year, lessons involved us just sitting under the tree and listening to the teacher, who had nothing to work with, but a blackboard and chalk. By the second year things had really got going though. A classroom had been built, and now we felt like we were the business. But it didn't stop there.

The school soon had a sceptic toilet, and that was the biggest development so far. It was a proper toilet with a sink and everything. None of us had ever seen a sceptic toilet before, and so the headmaster, Mr Christopher, arranged for a teacher to talk to the whole school and give us some training!

Everyone filed in to the hallowed bog, one by one, to be shown by the teacher how to sit on the toilet. We all had a crash course, which was much needed. Back home we used to just sit down and just 'pump' it down a little hole.

So while we were all shown how to sit on the toilet, using your bum, we found it hard not to crouch with our feet on the toilet seat. You can't change seven years of procedure overnight, so before long a sign appeared on the toilet door with the solemn instruction:

"EVERY BOY AND GIRL MUST SIT ON THEIR BUM WHEN USING THE TOILET."

But the sign didn't work. It felt so uncomfortable sitting on the seat. I, like most of my mates, just did my best to stand on the seat and balance, which was not the easiest thing to do because it was quite slippery. So in his frustration, Mr Christopher arranged for us all to come and see how it's done again, in groups of five girls and five boys; which we did. Imagine a 'year three' teacher in England trying to have a dump, while ten willing pupils huddled round and bombarded her with questions!

I nearly pissed myself when I recently found out that Mr Christopher's daughter now works in a toilet factory in Goroka. The struggle he had getting us to sit on a toilet must have had a profound effect on him!

And I'm afraid it wasn't all plain sailing from then on. Two weeks after the retraining, the toilet was closed because the sceptic tank had been blocked. It wasn't me. But all sorts of things must have been shoved down there. An official looking line of red and white tape showed that the fabled loo was out of bounds, and we were back to the pitch toilets at the boundary of the school. These toilets were on a piece of ground that the school didn't want to use, and after one year couldn't use anyway!

I suppose that took the pressure off us for a while. We were able to go to the toilet again on the comfort of our own two feet. Even now, the only sceptic toilet in the village is in my house. Maybe I should put a big WC sign on it when I'm away!

I grew up with pitch toilets. I guess 'toilet' is stretching the point a little. It was actually a hole in the ground. But we did build a hut around it to stop the rain getting in. Even so, for a little kid crawling around, they were very dangerous. And sometimes I went to the toilet to find that a pig had fallen down. Not every pig likes to be in shit! But having said that, it was a sure fire way for a pig to avoid the chop if a celebration was due.

The holes had to be big, because they needed to last a long time. And they were never emptied. When they got full, we filled them in, moved the hut and dug another one. Kaula said you could always see where an old toilet was, by looking for the best tomatoes!

♦

Soon after I first arrived in England to play for Rovers, I was invited for dinner by a lovely couple called Terry and Liz. They were big fans of Hull KR and really generous people. And so one weekend they had offered to cook a meal for me and a couple of their friends.

I was a bit nervous when I first went into their house. It was in a nice area of Hull that I hadn't been to before, and when I went inside, the hallway and lounge were really smartly decorated and very clean. It was grander than my flat on Holderness Road for sure, and for that matter anywhere else I'd seen. But as the evening went on I started to feel more relaxed, the food was great and Terry was making sure that my glass was full.

I felt quite pleased with myself, although I couldn't speak very good English, I didn't think I was letting myself down and I was trying to be as polite as I could to Terry and Liz's friends. I thought to myself how proud Kaula and Maul would be of me, having a meal with a group of white people, and knowing what to do. It was a few weeks after I'd been for dinner at Crooksy's house so I hadn't been to the Lucky Star beforehand and the evening was going very well.

After the main course, which was a fantastic lasagne, I excused myself to go to the toilet. And this was going to be one of those occasions where my training back at primary school, under Mr Christopher's expert guidance, was going to come to fruition. I didn't know everything about life in England but I certainly knew how to sit on a toilet.

But then on entering the bathroom, I couldn't believe my eyes. There were two toilets, one of which was about normal height, and the other which was lower down. I later found out that the lower one was a bidet, although I still don't know what that is, but I do know it isn't a toilet. At that moment though, I was still excited by the new experiences that I was having every day and so I naturally tried out the lower 'bog'. What a great country.

It wasn't all that comfortable and I actually had to crouch in any case, just like back at school. But then the next horror hit me. I turned the tap on but hardly any water gushed out to flush away my huge turd. Instead a little sprinkle of water just made it a bit sloppier. The only thing I could think was to grab handfuls of toilet roll and scrape the mess I'd made, out of the low level toilet and into the bigger one that had a conventional flush. I was halfway through this unpleasant manoeuvre when there was a knock on the door:

"Is everything okay in there Stan, are you alright?"

Terry was the perfect host and he was worried that I'd been away for quite a while. So I hurriedly stuffed the paper down the toilet and went back into the dining room, leaving clear signs of my struggle in three of the four pieces of the bathroom suite.

Before the evening was out Liz asked me how my digestive system was adapting to English food. It was then that I wondered if Mr Christopher's toilet training at school had actually been any use after all!

◆

My friends from primary school are still my best mates now. I get in touch with them every time I go home. They're all into the rugby and follow what I'm doing, and it's always great to see them. My three closest pals were Robin, who's now a teacher, Keith, who was actually called Lulu, and Tony. Keith changed his name when he was a bit older because he thought Lulu was shit. And I suppose he was right. That's why I always call him Lulu when I see him now.

We had great days at school. I've heard people over here sometimes say that your schooldays are the best days of your life, and I can see why. I couldn't say that for sure myself, because I am still stunned by what's happened to me throughout my life, and so it's hard for me to say when the best days actually were. But we certainly had fun at school.

Not that there was any lack of discipline. Mr Christopher was a hard man. And he was determined that all his pupils would grow up with an education and a respect for their elders. He also inspired fear in the guilty, because he had a one metre length of hose, which someone told me he called 'Harry', and he used it to whip kids who'd been bad, on their hand or, even worse, on their arse.

At the back of the school there was a united church. The church is still there now. But the really interesting thing for us was that behind the church there was a mini banana plantation, and a hang house in the church. The hang house was a place where bunches of bananas that had been chopped down were hung to ripen. They hung there until they were just right and ready to sell. And these were a different kind of banana. They were a sort of hybrid, and bigger than normal, and they tasted really good.

So obviously they were too tempting for us to resist. It was Lulu who first saw them, and it wasn't long before we were all sneaking round the church at lunchtime, to steal the bananas, and stuff them in our lunch bags. This, we thought, was a fantastic scam and the perfect crime. But at the age of seven our criminal minds had not fully developed. In fact we were quite stupid.

Instead of taking all the bananas with us back to school, we started eating them as soon as we'd nicked them. And so over time, a trail of banana skins, from the back of the church to our playground started to appear.

At lunchtime all the kids used to sit with their class in a circle, or a semicircle and eat or swap their lunch. And for many weeks Tony, Lulu, Robin and I had been proudly eating our hybrid bananas.

This particular day, the teacher had rung the bell and we all ran out to the playground and formed our circle. We were happily munching away, when Tony noticed the pastor, who we didn't often see, was outside the school talking to Mr Christopher. He gave me a dig in my rib:

"Hey man, what do you think the pastor wants with Mr C?"

"I don't know bro, but he's not looking too happy. Maybe he wants the school to be moved."

It was a wild guess, and nowhere near the truth. And soon we were shuffling, rather more uncomfortably, as a very serious looking priest walked over to us accompanied by Mr Christopher, who spoke to us with a disturbing smile:

"Good afternoon gentlemen. I hope you are all enjoying the lunches that your loving mum's have prepared for you. Open your boxes boys; let's see what you have to eat today."

He slowly turned full circle, peering into the twenty open lunch boxes, and then he said:

"Hmm, nice bananas boys. Tony, Keith, Stanley and Robin, can you come to my office to see me?"

Well this was a surprising twist. Until now, the only time we had been told to go to the headmaster's office was when we'd done something good. And we tried to think why we were going to get our praise. And Mr Christopher was smiling and talking really nicely to us, so we couldn't have done anything wrong. As we trooped over, I said to Lulu:

"Hey bro, do you think we're going to get some sweets?"

Not exactly, as it turned out. Had we been old enough to understand the rules of crime and punishment, we would probably have known what was coming.

And boy did it come. Whack! Harry the hose swished down on us with frightening expertise. And I tell you what, for a few seconds you don't feel any pain and then … stinging, burning agony! Jeez, I can still remember the pain now and it makes my eyes water. But also it was embarrassing to get hit in front of all the other kids. I know there's always stuff in the papers over here, with people moaning that when kids are bad, they just get an 'ASBO badge'. And there's this politically correct stuff that says if you hit a kid, he'll be mentally affected. Well I tell you what. I was mentally affected. So much so, that I didn't steal any more bananas.

♦

We didn't have any equipment to play with at school, no footballs or rugby balls or anything, so we made our own games, and things to play with. We could make a ball by getting a load of plastic bags, squeezing them together, then wrapping sticky tape around them. But they didn't last that long. If we wrapped a load of elastic bands around it, we could make a smaller, better ball that we could throw around. And with that, we could play our favourite game, 'the tin game'.

The tin game was a seven-a-side game, where each team stood either side of a wall of old tins, five at the bottom, four on top, then three, two and one to make a kind of pyramid. You threw the ball back and forwards at each other, and if the other team knocked the wall down, then you had to build it back up, before you were hit by the ball. Otherwise you were out. So if your team had the ball, they'd throw it a long way to give you a chance to build the wall. Have you got that? It was brilliant.

Rather less brilliant was jacket fighting. This involved two people taking their jackets off and hitting each other with them. Actually, come to think of it, maybe Sky would be interested in that one, a kind of celebrity jacket fighting. You'd certainly pay to see Peter Andre jacket fighting with Geoff Capes wouldn't you? It'd be much more exciting than the Premiership. And you could have tag jacket fighting with the Top Gear team against those posh girls from 'What not to Wear'. You could even improve the X Factor final by changing the public vote to a jacket fight. They wouldn't even have to sing. I must make a note of that one.

Jacket fighting was actually banned in our school, after some kid got a nasty cut on his head when he was hit with a denim jacket. I thought that was a bit hasty, they could have just banned the use of denim.

It has to be said that injuries were quite common during our games. But isn't it often the case that the best games are just a little bit dangerous? We had one game where we used our measuring rulers to shoot nuts that had fallen from the tree. The rulers were made out of bamboo because it was very strong. It was stripped off, cut, and then we etched the markings with a knife. But it was also very, very bendy. You could hold a nut on the end of the ruler, bend it back, let it go and the nut would go like a bullet. So when the teacher turned his back, nuts would be flying around like missiles.

One day in the playground at recess, Lulu sent an absolute rocket, just as this kid called Donald turned his head. And the nut shot straight into his ear. There was pandemonium and everybody panicked. Kids were trying to get it out, putting their fingers in Donald's ear, and he was crying his eyes out. Every time you put your hand in, the nut just went further in. He said it was hurting so we had to think of something. Tony came up with a plan:

"Hey, why don't we blow down his ear, and the nut will fly out of the other side?"

We weren't absolutely sure that this would work … but it was worth a try. So we held Donald still while one by one, we took a huge breath and blew as hard as we could down his ear. Poor old Donald was now howling because it was really painful. Tony looked in his other ear and shouted:

"It's working Stan! Keep blowing, keep blowing."

Five minutes later we had run out of breath. And close examination of both ears didn't tell us where the nut had got to. Donald was still sniffling and so we thought it best to get adult help. We needed someone with a lot of puff.

As it turned out it was even worse than we thought. Donald had to go to hospital to get the nut out, but we didn't know how they did it.

The next week we had a visit to the school from an APO, we didn't know what that stood for but he was kind of like a doctor who was an expert in accidents. And he showed us a diagram of a head with the ear channels. It didn't have a gap between the ears, and so I guessed that our attempts at blowing a nut right through were never actually going to work. We had learned something useful that day.

And all's well that ends well. Donald is now a policeman in Goroka … although he is deaf in his right ear. So if you're ever getting mugged it's always helpful to be on his left side!

♦

Our teacher in the first, second and third grades was Mr Harris, and what a great guy he was. When I'm over here in England I can still picture his face clearly. In fact I saw him when I went home last year. He always speaks to me and tells me stories about what's going on back home now. He was a really big influence on me.

And he was a fantastic character. He would always join in with us. If someone had come up with a new game, he was nearly always there to come and try it out. And he had some great ideas himself. I don't remember ever seeing him jacket fighting though.

Mr Harris was a fine figure of a man. He was very sporty and distinguished, with a long beard and lots of frizzy hair. He still has the beard now, although it's gone grey. I look back at him as a friend, but at the time he held the future of our education in the palm of his enormous hand.

He was a really funny guy and a very clever teacher. I remember one day, as we were packing our bags to go home, he said:

"Okay boys and girls. What I want you to do for your homework tonight is to go and see who can find the best pineapple, and bring it into school tomorrow."

We worshipped Mr Harris, and to get a task like this was really exciting. So we all rushed home, and as soon as we got there we went foraging in our grandmas' and granddads' gardens looking for the best pineapple. It never occurred to us that our folks had worked hard to grow the best fruit, and that they'd get good money for it at the market. Oh no, we were focussed on only one thing; getting the best pineapple for Mr Harris.

The next morning we all took our pineapples in, full of anticipation. And then he'd walk around the class with a big sack saying, 'thank you, thank you, thank you' as we dropped them in one by one. That was the last we saw of the pineapples. I sort of realise that he shouldn't have been doing that now, but Mr Harris was our God, and we'd do anything that he asked.

Homework was always different and interesting. We did a lot of work understanding about nature, agriculture and how subsistence workers could live off the land. And Mr Harris had a great way of illustrating what he was teaching us about. One day we'd been learning about the different trees and plants in the rainforest and he had another exciting assignment for us:

"Okay kids, you've all worked really hard today, so what I want you to do for your homework tonight is for each of you to get a bamboo, and bring it in to me tomorrow. Good afternoon everyone and be safe."

So, as always, we charged home, each of us determined to get the best possible bamboo for Mr Harris. Dads and granddads could be seen all evening combing through the bush, with their kids, all searching for an acceptable quality of bamboo. There was a lot of excitement, and a sort of community mission, even though we all wanted to be the best.

The next morning Mr Harris turned up with a pick up truck, and we all dutifully threw our bamboos into the back. Then he hooked the back of the truck up and drove off. Of course it turned out that Mr Harris was building a chicken house, and using the bamboo to weave the roof. This for me was yet more evidence that as well as enriching the mind, learning can be valuable in many ways.

But more than anything, Mr Harris was a brilliant teacher. There was nothing he didn't know about all three of our main subjects, maths, English and agriculture. And he did a lot for us all, and he's the only teacher I still keep in touch with. He took us right through to the fourth grade, when Mrs Matthews became our teacher. She was very clever and really nice, but she had an awful lot to live up to.

♦

Our happy, carefree school days were always going to come at a cost though. Not only in terms of the money, but at the end of primary school there was a big task facing us all. Aged ten or eleven, we had to sit an exam, to see whether we could go onto high school. Not the best high school, any high school at all. Because if we failed that was it, the end of our education. And there were no two ways about it. It was brutal. Fail at age ten, and then there was nothing to do, but work on the land when you were old enough.

Looking back now I think it's a disgrace. We have a government that spouts on about education and then throws thousands of ten year old kids on the scrap heap every year. There are no secondary schemes, no apprenticeships, nothing.

So on the final day at the end of the school year, every kid who'd reached the sixth grade sat the same exam. It was mainly maths, English and general knowledge. I had done quite well at school, I was good at maths and I often won prizes at the end of the year. But when I sat down to do the exam; I knew that this was the point of no return. If I was sick, or had a block, then I was history. It was like taking a penalty from right in front of the posts. There's no way that you can miss. But … there is always that slight chance. There was always the slight chance that I'd end up hearing someone uttering Eddie Waring's immortal words:

"He's missed it …. He's missed it …. the poor lad."

It was always a worry at the back of my mind. But come results day the worry was over. There were parents and kids at the school picking up their results, some smiling broad smiles, some crying. It's not a nice thing to go through for anyone. And when kids over here talk about the pressure of exams, when they're already guaranteed a grade through their coursework, thanks to the internet, it's a bit like premiership footballers talking about pressure, when League Two players can lose their house if they get relegated.

Robin and Tony passed the exam. And so did I. And so did Lulu. And now the big wide world awaited us all. Thank God, and thank Mrs Matthews. But most of all thank Mr Harris.

6

From Hull and back.

2000 - 2001
Hull F.C.

No matter what job you do, you always want to test yourself at the highest level possible. If you enjoy your work, but you think you can do better, then it's natural to want to swim in new waters. That's what I kept telling myself at the end of the 1999 season. It was an emotional time for me, and a very difficult one. I was really worried that I was biting the hand that had fed me so well in my first years in a new country. I remembered when I first arrived at Hull Kingston Rovers four years earlier. At the time I was both frightened and excited. And the club had calmed my fears, and kept my feet on the ground.

And of course it was only four years ago that I had left my home in New Guinea. My mum was distraught when I told her that I was leaving PNG to come to England. She had paid my way all the way through school, and she was determined that I'd become a teacher. But I had a chance to do what I loved the most and I took it. Even Mum would admit now that it was the right thing to do. And so now I convinced myself that I had to carry on trusting my instinct and convictions.

But I had enjoyed a fantastic time at Craven Park. And when I thought of the laughs I'd had, the friends I'd made, and the feelings that were still very strong to me, like when I was carried around the ground at Featherstone, it became all the harder to leave. But the deal had been done.

My agent, Derek, had phoned me about three quarters of the way through the previous season. He knew about the interest that St Helens had shown previously, and he also knew that I was desperate to reach the Super League with Rovers. But like any good agent he was hedging his bets:

"Hi Stan, how are you feeling at the minute?"

When your agent asks you a question like that, you know that he either has an offer that he wants to put to you, or he's looking to renegotiate his fees. But ever since I'd known Derek, he'd always been really good to me. And he was passed on by Paul Fletcher, so I wasn't hassled. In fact, I was pretty pleased to hear from him. He carried on:

"What do you think Rovers chances are this year?"

"I don't know." I said. Because I didn't.

"Well I've got an offer for you, and I think it's one that you should have a proper think about."

It was twenty years too late for Blankety Blank, and five years too early for 'I'm a Celebrity Get Me out of Here'. Apart from that Derek wasn't a shit agent so I was confident I wasn't going to end up in panto at the Bradford Alhambra!

As it turned out, Derek had wind of an approach that had been made to Rovers. It was from the chief executive of a new team that was being put together in Newcastle. Gateshead Thunder was going to enter the Super League in 2000, and had put the feelers out for players that could bring the crowds in. The club was being formed by a group of Australians, and they already had an Aussie coach called Shaun McRae in place. It turned out that I had first come to these guys' attention playing for the Kumuls in the 1995 World Cup, and they had been following my progress. I was pleased to have been considered, but at the same time I knew that this was my time. I knew that I was good enough to play in the top league, and so I agreed to speak to Gateshead's representatives.

But first I wanted to speak to Hull KR. Just as I had sat down with my mum before I left PNG to come to Hull in the first place. I didn't want to go through the same tears and hugs this time, and I wasn't disappointed. If you ever want be sure of a completely manly farewell, do it with rugby people.

Derek had already done all the groundwork, and I also found out that the Gateshead Thunder chief executive had already spoken to the Hull KR board. I guess it was all done in the right order, but I was the last one to consider the deal. So when I had decided to go, that was it. I sat down with Phil Lowe and Colin Hutton in the boardroom, and while there was a big part of me that felt bad that I was asking to leave, they made it easy for me. I think that Phil in particular understood my reasons.

There was no other way I could say it, partly because there was no point in beating about the bush, but also because my language still wasn't perfect. So I could easily have ended up beating around the wrong bush:

"I want to play for Gateshead."

Colin was quick to reassure me: *"Look, we know Stan. And listen, you've done a grand job for us here. We've spoken to Gateshead. If you think it's the right thing for you to…*

"You can piss off with our blessing!" Phil finished the sentence. *"It's about time someone else can see what you do."*

It was a bit like Gordon Ramsay telling me I'd made a good omelette, but it was time for me to learn how to kill a lobster. So no tears and hugs then. I wondered why I'd been so nervous. I went to tell Dave Harrison, the coach, and that was that.

In many ways I was relieved to get this all sorted out, and when I signed my two year contact, I knew it was all going to happen. And for me it was great to be playing for a newly formed team, it added to the excitement. And I knew there would be a lot of telly matches.

There had been some rumours the year before that I was maybe going across the city to play for Hull F.C. I had said categorically 'no' but you can't stop some people believing what they want. So I could put this to bed once and for all. And the Hull Daily Mail had a big picture of me under the Humber Bridge, eating a bag of fish and chips. The story line was basically 'told you so …. I said I would never go across to the other side.'

I was quite happy with that.

♦

As soon as I had got the nod, I had to talk to Jo. That was going to be a bit more difficult. Elliott was nearly three, and I didn't know if it would be unsettling for him. But Jo told me that if this was a big chance for me to get on with my career, then she was right behind me. I knew by now, of course, that Jo was going to be a part of me forever, and so it was always important that we planned things together.

We drove up to Newcastle one weekend to have a look around, and it seemed like a good city to me. Plenty of Chinese takeaways and it was actually no colder than Hull. It was just bloody freezing. So I felt better after that. We also went to look at the Gateshead Stadium, which looked fantastic to me. It had been the home to Gateshead Harriers for ages, and I knew that they were the best athletics club around. So they had the best facilities. We drove home happy, also because it wasn't all that far from Hull. And I thought that Jo would want to be near to her parents.

That was also good news for me, because from the first meeting, and the welcome I'd had, I always felt that Paul and Stephanie were family to me too. They had done too much for me. And they'd been brilliant for me in so many ways. I'm convinced that they helped me to settle down and feel at home as much as Jo did.

Over the next couple of weeks, as we talked about it more and more, one or two complications started to appear. The main one was that Jo would have to find a job in Newcastle. At the time she was a teaching assistant, and I knew that she loved her work. I didn't want to drag her away from that, but I thought there must be a solution, particularly as Newcastle was so close.

Eventually, we agreed that to start with, I'd go up and live in Newcastle and every weekend, I'd go and see Jo and Elliott or pick them up and we could all go to Newcastle. It would only be to start with, and it would also give Jo time to get used to the idea. When the summer term came, she could give her notice, and then look for a job in Newcastle. In the meantime she could spend her time between our house on Leads Road and her mum and dad's. It wasn't ideal, but it seemed like the best thing to do to begin with. And it made some sense for me to be able to concentrate fully on my footy, now that I was heading for the Super League.

So the weekend before the new season started, we borrowed a van, and took enough of my stuff up for me to be able to move in; noticeably my guitar, my wardrobe of stylish clothes and my wok (which I hadn't actually used).

The house that the club had set up for me was on a cul-de-sac, and there were three other houses. It looked to me like Brookside Close! They were all owned by a property guy, I think he was a farmer as well. Gateshead Thunder had rented them all to put some of the players in. I guess that was to give us all a chance to get to know each other. It had to be good for team spirit, unless we all hated each other's domestic habits of course!

I was moving into a house next to Wayne MacDonald. This really was the big time for me. Not the house sharing part. Wayne had played for Leeds Rhinos and Saints, and he was a household name. One of my mates told me he's living in Dubai now. I think he's a fitness trainer. Paul Broadbent, the Wakefield assistant coach, had a house there too. At the time, he'd just left Sheffield Eagles.

◆

Pre-season training was going well. We trained down at the Gateshead stadium and everything felt right. It was a magnificent setting and it inspired the players and coaches to give everything they had. There was a real vibrancy about the team and the club as a whole. This was fresh, we were full of ambition, and there was a sense of stepping out into the unknown. I couldn't wait for the season to start, and I was training as hard as I ever had.

At weekends I was going down to see Jo and Elliott. And every weekend was special. I think when you work hard all the way through the week, there's nothing better than spending time with your family at the weekend. I knew that once the season started, this would be more difficult, so I made the most of the chances I had.

We'd been training for four weeks and the first match was only two weeks away, and I'd just had a great weekend with Jo. Monday training always started at nine so I set my alarm for quarter past eight. But I was woken by the ring tone of my mobile at seven. I guessed it had to be Jo. Who else would be ringing me at that time? I looked at the phone with bleary eyes. It wasn't Jo:

"Yeah ..... who is it?"

It was Shane Richardson, the chief executive from the club.

"Hi Stan, get yourself down here mate. There's a players meeting at eight. Make sure you're not late."

And that was it. No explanation. Nothing. It was a freezing morning and I wasn't best pleased to have missed over an hour of my beauty sleep. But as I wearily dressed myself and shuffled out to the car, a dark realisation started to creep over me.

I'd heard some rumours that Gateshead might be merging with Hull. When I was down at the weekends, Paul Westmorland, one of my best Hull KR mates had said that Hull F.C. were in financial trouble. And the early signs in Newcastle suggested that there might not be as much interest in Super League as they had hoped. The rumours of a merger were very strong in Hull. I had asked Shane about it but he was adamant that it wouldn't happen.

Surely not? It had to be something else. I hadn't pissed on the Pope, as far as I knew, so why on earth would anyone do that to me?

Up at the stadium we all sat in a circle. All the guys were there, and we were pumping Tony Grimaldi, the captain, for information. But Tony didn't know any more than we did. I said to the boys, jokingly, that we're all going back to Hull, and then Shane came in.

Before he said anything he looked at me and shook his head. Oh shit. Sure enough, he was about to deliver the chilling truth:

"Boys, we're going to Hull."

I felt my stomach drop through the bottom of my pants, and then wiz back up. No …. no, no , no. I thought back to the time that Mr Christopher had asked us into his office, after we were caught stealing bananas. Maybe God was still punishing me. The first thing that came to my mind was that I was now going to hurt the supporters who had loved me, and who I had loved for four years.

I rang my friend Paul straight away. I wanted to confess what was happening, to one of my best mates, as soon as I could. He kind of put me at ease. He's a proper Hull bloke. He said:

"Get on Stan. Just get on with it. It's a job. If I got sacked by one shipping company, I'd just go and look for another shipping company. Sometimes you have to do work you don't really want to mate."

He was right in what he said, but I know he didn't really mean it from his heart. I think he probably felt a bit sorry for me, because he knew how much the Rovers meant to me.

♦

Jo had quit her job already, because we didn't want to wait for the summer for her to move up to Newcastle. But thankfully, she got it back. I know she's really good at her work and the school would have been sorry to lose her. We moved my stuff back into our house on Leads Road. And at least we could settle down again here, in Jo's home town, and my UK home. We had a quiet night in on my first day back. A bottle of wine and a Chinese takeaway then Jo went upstairs. I was a bit restless and I was flicking around to see if I could catch a late night film. 'Sleeping with the Enemy' was on Channel 4, so I went to bed.

Once the shock of the past week had subsided, I got on with my job. I was still completely focussed on what I wanted to achieve. Alright, I was going to be playing for Hull at the Boulevard, but it was still in the Super League. And when I thought about everything, that's where I really wanted to be.

In pre-season training I didn't have the whole hearted support of all the fans though. I was subjected to some rapier-like wit from the sidelines, like 'get back to Rovers you dickhead!' They must have stayed up all night thinking that one up. I don't think the Hull Daily Mail helped. They printed a picture of me, in exactly the same pose as before, under the Humber Bridge, but this time wearing the black and white Hull F.C. shirt. I thought of the 'Magnificent Two Hundred' in Wales, and the lads who carried me around the ground at Featherstone. The Rovers fans hadn't taken it too well. And I felt like shit.

And of course Jo and I had to move out of the house that Hull KR provided for us! I guess that was only right. So we moved in with Paul and Stephanie. We still call it our favourite hotel to this day. And in all the upheaval and uncertainty I had in my professional life, I think it was kind of comforting.

Our first game was a friendly against Halifax. And thank God I had a good one. The whole team worked well together, and we won easily. I scored a try and I was the sponsors' 'man of the match'. I had heard some abuse at the start of the game, but nothing in the second half. The way I'd played and the response I got from the crowd had given me confidence. It had been my first game for Hull, but hearing someone in the crowd shout, 'go on Stan!' was a big thing for me. After all, I was still in a foreign country and acceptance was and is always important.

The Super League season kicked off, and I was a bit disappointed to find myself on the bench at the start. Shaun said to me that it was my first season in Super League and I should try to come into the game step by step and not take things too quickly. Seemed fair enough. When I came on I was doing okay, and I was getting a good reaction from the crowd. Sometimes I heard supporters shouting at Shaun to get me on, so I knew that a good section of the Hull crowd was backing me.

And it was definitely exciting. The crowds were massive and often we were playing in front of 20,000 people. I was coming up against the best teams in the country, Bradford Bulls and Leeds Rhinos. And I was playing against some of the best players in the world, Barrie McDermott and all the New Zealand lads at Leeds, and Henry and Robbie Paul at Bradford.

But for all the wide eyed excitement, I wasn't completely happy. Sure, I was in the Super League, but I wasn't doing exactly what I wanted to do. That was to play eighty minutes every week. I understood that this was a different level, but after all it was the same game. And I knew that I was playing well enough to make a bigger contribution. At the same time I could see lots of good players around me, and lots of promising players coming through; the likes of Paul Cooke, Richard Horne and Paul King were all giving Shaun a headache.

The team finished in a respectable mid table position and I decided to see what the next year would bring. After all, I still had another year of my contract to run.

♦

In the close season I went home to PNG as usual. But this time I had a job in mind. Some years earlier, Maul and Kaula had moved out of the village and into the settlement about five minutes walk away. It was a sort of a ghetto, but it was a good place for Maul and Kaula to go. When Kaula retired from his job at the hospital, he used his retirement money to buy a little shop in the settlement where we all could live. He also bought a house for his second wife.

I didn't have much to do with Kaula's second wife. It wasn't at all unusual for guys of his age to have two wives, but the whole set up didn't seem quite right to me. She seemed a good enough woman, but I often wondered what Maul thought of it all.

A week before the flight I rang my mum, Christina, to let her and my two brothers know that I was on the way. My little brother Ben was sixteen now and baby Martin was eleven. They had grown up while I had been in England. So I always looked forward to getting home to see them and to play some footy. Mum sounded hassled:

"Stanley, thank God you're coming home now. But there's something I need to tell you before you get here."

What the hell was coming here? She went on:
"Look Stanley, Kaula has taken a third wife."

"WHAAT? A third wife! Jesus, what's he doing? He's too old for this!" I think he was about seventy.

I could tell from Mum's tone of voice that she didn't need convincing. In her own way, Mum had stood up for women all her life. She wasn't one of those man–hating feminists you see over here. You know the type that spray rape gas in your eyes if you open the door for them, and don't shave their armpits. There are few worse situations than being temporarily blinded amidst a cloud of body odour! She was a proper woman, who showed strength and love in equal measures. She had the 'balls' to kick Robert out when he took a second wife all those years ago, and she worked all her life to support her family. She had a respected voice in the village. And Kaula could have done a lot worse than listening to her.

Maul wasn't cool about it either, but she had more to worry about in her life. Kaula wasn't getting any younger, and I think in the whole situation that's what worried her most. I'm sure that if she had been a younger woman she wouldn't have accepted it. Mum also told me that the third wife was a young girl, young enough to be Kaula's daughter, and she was calling round asking for money. I suppose that's one of the only times where you do see some similarities between life in PNG and the UK. The daft old sod.

But that annoyed me even more. Ever since I had been in England I had sent £100 a month over to Maul. It was enough to help her out for two months but I wanted to do it. But Maul used to share it with the old people in the village. I kept telling her that I sent it over for her and Kaula. But she just always said that it was a blessing.

While I was on the plane home I was building myself up for my confrontation with Kaula. I had a lot more confidence than when I had left home for the first time. But I was still nervous. And when I walked into his house I didn't really know what I was actually going to say. So it just came out anyway:

"What the hell are you thinking of Dad? What are you doing? Stop it! Stop it man. It's ridiculous. You're getting too old for all this kind of thing. All your mates will think you've gone mad. You can't go running around the village with a girl. She's less than half your age, it's bloody ridiculous you silly old git! She'll wear you out, you'll be knackered."

Kaula smiled at me:
"You're right son."

♦

I returned to Hull, as I always did, full of enthusiasm for the new season. I was refreshed and raring to go. After the worry of Kaula's goings on, back home everything was carrying on as normal. I had his assurance that he was sticking at three, and so there wasn't a lot more to say or do. And he would always be my dad, and I loved him whatever he did, because I owed him so much.

Hull F.C. is a great club, and back in 2001 they were very ambitious. I had seen plans for the new K.C. Stadium that was being built, and was looking forward to making my mark in the Super League. Sure, I had got a little frustrated in the first year, because I spent so much time sat on the bench. But I listened to what Shaun had to say, and understood where he was coming from. I was doing alright in training and I just wanted to see what the next season would bring. I was even talking to Derek about a contract extension, so on the whole I was happy where I was. But I desperately needed time on the pitch.

And when I had my chance, I was playing my guts out. But nothing seemed to have changed. I was getting ten minutes here, and twenty minutes there, and I honestly believed that I was playing well enough to get a start.

As the weeks rolled on it was beginning to eat at me. And because I didn't have the confidence to go in and speak to Shaun it was just snowballing up inside of me. The only person I spoke to was Jo. And she told me that I just had to sit down with Shaun and sort it out. I kind of felt sorry for her, because my growing anger was coming out at home. I know I was getting sulky, and Jo could see that I was getting more and more unhappy. It was bound to affect the whole of my life because rugby means so much to me. It's my job … it's the only thing that I do. I love it, and if I'm not doing it I'm not happy.

But it just carried on. I was coming off the bench, straining every muscle in my body and putting it on the line. Then being called back to the bench. It was starting to drive me nuts. I was being played all over the place, stand off, hooker, I was getting pushed into the back row, everywhere. But my confidence was being held up more often than not by the fans. Sitting on the bench at the Boulevard I could hear them shouting, 'Get Stan on, get Stan on' so I knew that I must be doing something right. The supporters had taken to me, which was a great thing, considering where I had come from. So why wasn't I getting a start? Now I know that's a question I should have asked Shaun.

I suppose that in any job that you do in life, the manager always has his favourites and some guys get on better than others. And it's not personal. One manager can see something in you, which another manager can't. It doesn't necessarily mean that one manager's better than the other. It just means that we all see things differently. And I kept myself calm by just telling myself that, over and over again.

Even when you're feeling down, there's always someone or something that can make you smile. And at Hull that was Billy Mallinson. He was a fitness trainer at the Boulevard, and a great kid. Our strength and endurance training was usually running up hills. It's difficult to find a hill in Hull, but Billy always seemed to manage it. But the thing about him that stays with me is that he was always smiling. And while I was at my lowest ebb, that made me smile. After all these years it's great to see Billy working at Craven Park now. He's one of those guys that can build you up, just by being the way he is.

I have no axe to grind with Shaun at all. He's a really nice guy to talk to. This in some ways makes it harder to understand why I never actually sat down with him, to talk about my worries, as Jo had said I should. But in his eyes I just wasn't good enough.

And let me get this straight. I would have stayed at Hull if I had been given a chance. As I said it's a great club with big ambitions, and fantastic support. And the supporters were good to me. After they'd got over where I'd come from I really felt that they had got behind me. There are always some arseholes who don't understand sport, but there are arseholes in every walk of life. Everybody knew even then that I was Rovers through and through. But I am a professional, and I was ready to give every ounce of my body for Hull.

But for whatever reason it just didn't work out. And I didn't know that as I was struggling to stake my claim for a place, Huddersfield Giants had been discussing a loan move for me, with the Hull board.

I don't have any single bad memory of my time at the Boulevard. The supporters were great and there were some really good people there. But in my heart of hearts, I didn't feel wanted. And when the chance came, I was ready to get out.

7

One Giant Step For Stan

2001 – 2003
Huddersfield

Every once in a while, something happens that sets your life on a different course. And it's usually completely out of your control. It can be someone watching you play a game, it might be walking into a shop at the same time as your future wife; or it could be a simple phone call.

This time it was my mobile ringing as I was on my way to the training ground on a miserable Monday morning. It was a number that I didn't recognise, and a voice that I didn't either, but it was Australian, so I guess that narrowed it down a little:

"Hi Stan, it's Tony Smith here. Don't worry mate, you don't really know me, but I wanted to have a chat."

I didn't know Tony personally, but I did know that he was the coach at Huddersfield Giants. He got to his point pretty quickly:

"Listen Stan, you know that we're struggling at the minute, and we need to bring some fresh blood in. How do you fancy playing eighty minutes a week for us?"

Obviously Tony had been looking around and he knew that I wasn't getting a start. 'Struggling' was a bit of an understatement though. I think the Giants had lost fifteen games on the bounce and they were heading straight out of the Super League. But he had hit the nail on my head. I was desperate to be playing eighty minutes every week and so Tony had said exactly the right thing.

For sure, even though it was still only May, the Giants were certain to be going down. And Hull was sat in a comfortable position. But when all things considered, I was still being offered Super League footy and I had absolutely no doubts in accepting his offer. I had given it my best shot at Hull and now I just wanted to leave. Funnily enough being a Rovers fan, I honestly thought Hull was going to be the team for me. I was in my prime and at the top of my game, or so I thought. But it wasn't, and if I had the chance to do it all again, I wouldn't actually have changed anything.

"Do you know any of the lads at Huddersfield?" Tony asked, *"I bet you know Steve McNamara."*

I'd heard of Steve, and I knew he was from Hull but I'd never met him. So Tony said that he'd get Steve to give me a ring and arrange to pick me up for training in the morning.

That was bloody quick! One minute I was wondering where I was going at Hull, the next I was waiting for a call from my new team mate. Tony, Shaun and the two boards had agreed a loan deal to take me to Huddersfield for the rest of the season, subject to my agreement. It seems like I was the last to know again. But I didn't care; I had been given a new challenge and that was exactly what I needed.

♦

I went to bed that night feeling just as excited as I did before my first game for Hull KR. Somehow a weight had been lifted off my shoulders. It's hard to explain why, because I was stepping into the unknown again. But I guess I was starting to get used to it. And I was more focussed on the positive side, than worrying whether I'd done the right thing. Apart from that, I wasn't in two minds anyway, there was no way I'd have said, 'no'.

Steve Macca picked me up at seven in the morning and we drove down to Huddersfield. It was an easy journey because we just clicked from the moment I got in his car. It was as if we'd known each other for years. We had a good laugh and it made me feel that I was on the right track again. It would turn out that Steve was going to be a big influence on me and a great friend.

And when we got to the ground, Tony came up to meet us. He opened me up right away, just by the way he was. He gave me a big hug and immediately I felt as if I was wanted again. This all seemed right to me and the spring came back into my step at that very moment. I could tell that this was a very friendly place to be, and it was Super League as well. There were some top players there at the time, David Lomax, Paul Reilly, and of course Macca. But for some reason they just weren't winning. So that took the pressure off me in many ways, and I was determined to do well for them; because they seemed like the kind of guys that deserved to be winning.

After the morning training, we went to watch a video. It was a good chance for me to see my new team mates in action. And so we all sat down and Tony started to talk. But then my phone rang. I didn't notice that Tony stopped talking and the players were all looking at me. It was Jo, so I just walked out of the room. I finished the call and walked back in again and Tony didn't say a word. But when the meeting ended, Macca grabbed me by the arm and said:

"For fuck's sake, what did you think you were doing Stan?"

It was then that I realised that I shouldn't have done it. I'd made the mistake of thinking that because Tony appeared to be more relaxed than anything I had seen at Hull, he wasn't deadly serious.

I soon had my chance to repay the faith that Tony had showed in me. And it was that faith that had given me an extra bit of strength and determination. We were playing London at home on the Saturday, and in the morning I was really keyed up.

Everything seemed right. It was a sunny day and I was full of anticipation when I got to the McAlpine Stadium. I had never played in as good a stadium as this as a home player. I think the weather brought a few more fans out. At kick off there were about 4000 in the crowd and they were making a good noise.

You often find that the siege mentality brings out the best in the real fans.

Eighty minutes later, it was more like a party atmosphere. Sure it had been a good game. But more importantly we had won, for the first time in three months. I'd scored a try, which always makes it even better, and it was the most I'd enjoyed a game for as long as I could remember.

♦

Jo could see that I was happy again, and she said that it was nice to see the 'old Stan' back. It had been a while since I'd taken her to a KFC for lunch! Footy was great fun for me again. And you know that when you're enjoying your game funny things can happen. After going fifteen matches without winning, we won four out of the next 6, and we didn't even notice that we were catching up. Unbelievably we went into the last game of the season with a chance of staying up.

It had come right down to the wire. And on the final day of the season, if we won our game, and Wakefield lost at Salford we were safe. And the omens were good as far as I could see. It was a lovely sunny day and we were at home to London again. It wasn't going to be easy because London had a good side and I think they were in the top six, but we were right up for it. And on a good day Salford would put thirty or forty past Wakefield, so it looked like, for the first time all season, our destiny was as good as in our own hands.

And amazingly we did it. We beat London again. We had made a miraculous recovery from the mid season, and everyone at the club, from Tony right down, had given their all, and there wasn't an ounce of energy left within a two hundred metre radius.

But at the final whistle the ground didn't erupt. There was no pitch invasion, no singing, and no music banging out from the public address. Everyone was waiting for the result to come in from Salford. They had kicked off late and we had an agonising five minutes, watching the fans with their radios to their ears, and we were just sitting on the grass, or standing around.

It was the weirdest thing I'd ever experienced in the game. Twenty guys just standing on the pitch, thinking of God knows what; their futures, their mortgages, what's going to happen next year ... and it was all in the lap of the gods. Some of the top players knew that they would get offers either way, but not everyone. And the fans all just stood there in a kind of trance. On the pitch we were waiting for the supporters to tell us what had happened. All sorts of things were going through my mind. Wakefield was on a bad run, and for Salford it was a 'nothing' game, so they could play without pressure. It seemed like we were all stood there for an eternity.

But then I saw an old guy in the stand put his radio in his pocket and turn towards the exit. I looked around and it was as if a big black cloud had dropped over the whole place. Macca had his head in his hands and I knew what had happened. Of course, it had been a 'nothing' game for Salford, but it looked like they just hadn't turned up. My mum, Kaula, Maul and a few of their mates could have beaten Wakefield!

Fuck. There was nothing else to say. So I went home.

♦

For the next few days I was gutted. I had really settled in at Huddersfield, and we had so nearly pulled off one of the greatest escapes of all time. But the league table never lies, and the Giants were destined for National League One. But I didn't know where I was going. I had really hoped that we were going to make it, because I thought I might get a contract to stay in Huddersfield. And being in that set up had given me a lot of confidence. Tony had moved me a long way forward, not just as a rugby player, but as a person as well. He is a brilliant coach, and has acute tactical awareness from any position on the pitch. But he also helped me in my day to day life. He took more care in helping me with my language, and how to get on, than anyone before him. He sat down with me and talked to me; he told me that I was a very clever rugby player and he gave me real confidence. After three months there, I could stand up in front of my team mates and talk, and they listened. That was unbelievable for me. I had been in the UK for six years but this was the biggest step I had taken.

I was out of contract now but I had a couple of offers on the table. Jo and I were planning a trip to Australia and PNG with Elliott, and I had it in mind that I needed to get sorted out before we left. I was kind of pleased that the decision had been taken out of my hands. The week after our final game Tony was on the phone to me:

"Hi Stan, you all set for your holiday yet? Listen mate, I hope you've had a good time here because I've loved working with you. You've done really well for us and I'm just sorry we didn't quite make it. Anyway, I was wondering mate, how do you fancy staying on for a year to help us bring the club back up?"

I didn't need to think about it for long. In the short time I'd been at Huddersfield, I'd made friends that could pull on my sense of loyalty. And I honestly believed, and still do, that Tony had saved me. I would rather be where I wanted, trying to get in the Super League, than where I didn't want to be, trying to stay in it. I felt settled again. So I went in to see Tony and I signed a two year contract.

One of the main reasons that I felt settled was Macca. He's a special guy. I spent a lot of time driving up and down the M62 with Steve, and he talked to me about a lot more than rugby. I give a lot of the thanks for where my life is now to Steve. He's a family guy and he was instrumental in getting me to think more about my future and my family. He even talked to me about how to get security, and what to do with my money. Sometimes it was like being stuck in the car with a financial advisor. But this was so important for me. I'd spent the last six years like a kid in a toy store before Christmas. I didn't really know how to handle my money properly, and there are always people willing to take advantage of that. Steve gave me a lot of good advice.

He told me to spend more time with family as well. When you're twenty odd years old, that's not quite as obvious as it is now. And to have someone take the time to point me the right way was a gift. Don't get me wrong, I still have some spectacular blow outs, ask the hotel managers after our visit to Catalans last year, but I know now that there's a lot more to life.

I'd first heard of Macca when I was at Hull KR and he was at Bradford Bulls. He scored a lot of points and he was a great kicker. I used to watch the games in the pub and I noticed him because whenever he scored, they always played this song that ended, 'Ohhh McNamara!' I think it was that holiday song that has a stupid dance with it – the Macarena or something.

◆

With my future settled, I could now take Macca's advice and concentrate some time on my family. And Jo, Elliott and I had just planned the holiday of a lifetime. We were going to head down to Australia, to see the Great Barrier Reef, before going up to PNG to tour the island and then spend time with my family. Elliott was so excited. He was four now, and I guess he didn't really know where we were going to, but he wanted to get involved in all the packing, and was in and out of the suitcases, while Jo tried to keep control.

It was a cold December evening, and I was really looking forward to setting off. I kept saying to Jo, 'two days from now we'll be sunning ourselves by the barbeque'. I just couldn't wait; I think I was running around more than Elliott! We were flying from Manchester to Washington, and then had a connecting flight right down to Australia. And I always love it when the plane takes off, because I know then that I'm on my way. But on this occasion we had to wait, the plane was delayed by four hours. Oh well, four hours wasn't the end of the world, and it gave me more time to run around the airport with Elliott while Jo read a book.

You have to remember that this was December 2001. Only two months after the attacks on the World Trade Centre in New York. The tragedy that tore the heart out of Manhattan had lasting effects on the whole world, in the way that we all now look at each other with suspicion, if we don't come from the same country. And for 'suspicion' in the rest of the world, read 'neuroses' in America. The country that has catapulted psychotherapy into its status as a top profession is now obsessively looking around nervously for the next attacker that 'doesn't understand it'. For sure, the bombing was a truly horrific and terribly sad event, and you can understand how it might change people.

Of course, none of this was in my mind as we eventually took off from Manchester. We had a seven hour flight ahead of us and were due to arrive in Washington at four in the morning. Jo carried on reading her book while Elliott and I watched Pocahontas.

But when we arrived at Washington, you could sense the tension in the airport. I have to say that the videos they were showing of US senators speaking, interspersed with bomb explosions didn't lighten the atmosphere. At this very moment it didn't seem like a holiday any more, and we had the added hassle of sorting out a connecting flight to Los Angeles, as we had missed our plane to Australia. But it was when we reached the immigration desk that things started to get a bit tricky.

The guy on the desk, who was wearing a smart military uniform, had successfully got thumb imprints from Jo and Elliott, checked their passports, and ascertained the 'purpose of their visit' when it was my turn. Now my PNG passport does look a bit dodgy I must admit, certainly not up to scratch if you compare it with Jo's UK passport. That seemed to be enough for the security guy to test me a bit further. He fixed me with a determined stare. If he had been wearing a rugby shirt I would have smacked him, but he wasn't:

"Sir if you're travelling internally in the US today you'll need a Visa. Could I see your Visa please sir?"

We hadn't expected to be flying internally, if our flight hadn't been delayed from Manchester we would have been in the sky right at that moment. So I didn't have a Visa. I just had the good old PNG passport, which incidentally looked like I'd made it myself, crapped on it, and then put it through the washing machine. Unfortunately, I chose honesty to be the best policy:

"I haven't got one."

At least I thought that's what I said. But in the light of what happened next I think I must have said, 'you look a complete dick in that hat.' Sergeant Bilko pressed the alarm and I was dragged away by two much bigger guys, albeit in the same smart uniform. From there I was dumped into a small room with two chairs and a table in it. This wasn't funny any more. In fact it was quickly becoming a nightmare. And the worst thing was, that I could see, out of the window, Elliott and Jo were in another room, both crying their eyes out. Thank Christ Guantanamo Bay wasn't yet in the public eye, otherwise I would have shit my pants.

I sat in the room for three hours. It was dreadful. Even though it seemed like it was the middle of the night, it was stifling and sweaty, and I was scared to death, not knowing what had happened to Jo and Elliott. Every now and then these guys came in to ask me questions, about where I came from, where I got my money from and stuff like that. Then at about seven o'clock and without any warning I was taken out of the room and marched to the departure area, where I met Jo and Elliott. We hugged each other and checked that we were all ok, and then amazingly we were put on the plane to LA. I couldn't believe it. I wanted to look strong for Jo's sake but inside I was shaking. Thank God that was over. Soon we would be on our way to Australia and out of this shit hole.

But I'd underestimated the length that these people would go to, in extending their hospitality. As soon as we wandered into the arrival area at LA, we were met by another security guard, and his mates, who led us to a car, in which we were driven to a nearby hotel. Jo was frantic and poor little Elliott didn't know what the hell was going on. But for the first time in this bizarre situation, someone told us what was happening. Our flight from LA to Sydney was in ten hours, until which time we would be held in the hotel under armed guard, presumably for the security of the nation, rather than our own safety. I have to say, I was starting to wonder just how mental this whole country was.

Our personal 'minder' checked in with us at the reception, and accompanied us to our room, where our bags were thrown in, and it was there that we would have to wait for the next eight hours. Jo was looking really tired by this time, and she held the door open for our security man to leave. But he just sat down, right in front of the telly. I think this was as much as Jo could take. She had been crying for most of the morning, and she was just left with tearful and venomous anger. Now if Jo had shouted at me the way she shouted at the security guy, I would have left. But not only was he a professional, he was also Mexican and couldn't speak one word of English. This was going to be an absolute scream, frazzled wife, frightened son, and a heavily armed and silent baboon sat on a chair next to the bed!

After ten minutes of remonstrations, Jo to minder, Jo to me, me to minder and Elliott to everyone, we sat down for a rest. This had to be the strangest situation I had ever been in, and I fully expected to wake up at any moment. But while I was daydreaming, Jo was swinging into action. She made a call to reception, and shortly after an altogether calmer exchange, with the help of an interpreter, our bulky Mexican friend moved his chair outside the room onto the corridor.

I immediately felt the atmosphere lighten, and tried to make Jo laugh:

"Great, he's fallen for our plan, now's our chance to escape!"

Jo looked at me wearily:
"Shut up Stan."

Well, the room was a little less crowded, but we now only had one chair, so I paced around, wondering how we could pass the next seven hours. Sleep wasn't really on the cards, although Elliott was doing ok, and I was starving. Then across the street, I spotted something familiar. That big picture of the grey haired guy who looks like a creepy uncle, and the six foot red neon letters, K F C. Fantastic, it was a comfort to see that this bloody country had something English in it. Family Bucket here I come!

But I'd forgotten the terms of our accommodation. As I opened the door and set off down the corridor, Mexican minder showed that he had been kidding all along, and demonstrated his full grasp of our language. He grabbed me by the arm and bellowed in his best Schwarzenegger:

"NOOOO!"

It was at that point, that I vowed to myself, that when we finally got out of this mess, I would never set foot on this God forsaken country again. And I won't.

♦

So after our little hiccup in the US, we finally arrived in Australia. And it made everything seem worthwhile. For the first time in ten months I could feel the sun on my back, and this was going to be the holiday of a lifetime. I was determined that Jo and Elliot were going to have a great time. And after four days in Australia, our past ordeals were well and truly behind us. We went to Cairns, and then to see the Great Barrier Reef. We went on a glass bottom boat and saw the incredible and beautiful reef, and fish of all sizes and colours. Elliott was just wide eyed everywhere we went. We had just enough time to completely chill out, and 'stick another shrimp on the barby', before setting off on the next leg of our journey. We were relaxed and happy. Just the frame of mind I wanted to be, going home to see my family.

And when we reached Goroka, Elliott got the 'first time home' treatment, just as I had, and Jo had before him. It was just unbelievable to watch him. I don't think I saw him walking for the first two days, because every time someone put him on the floor, someone else just picked him up. And he made friends with the little kids in the village straight away.

Elliott was speaking English, and the other kids were speaking pidgin.
But they were getting on like a house on fire. I don't know how kids manage to do that. They seem to be able to understand different languages, and they don't have the same reservations that the grown ups do. In more ways than one. When Elliott saw that all the kids didn't have clothes on, he wanted to be like

them. So first he threw all his clothes out and then took his sandals off. It seemed weird to me, and Jo was really worried about him, but he just wanted to be one of the boys.

And very soon he was doing stuff that I did when I was a kid. One morning he cheerfully announced to me that he was going with the kids to the swimming pool. I knew straight away that it would be the little hole down by the creek, where kids jumped in on a hot day. Along with the pigs of course, who would cool off and drink in the 'pool'. So I said to him right away:

"Now listen to me Elliott. You can play with the kids, but you mustn't jump into the pool. It's very dirty. Have you got that?"

Elliott nodded his reply and ran out of the door. A few minutes later when I explained to Jo where he'd gone, she was mad:

"Oh Stan, for goodness sake! How could you let him go? He's four years old. He'll get typhoid or malaria or something. I can't believe it."

"Don't worry Jo, he'll be fine. I told him not to jump in."

Jo gave me one of those looks that doesn't need any words to go with it. The look itself can let you know that you've dropped a huge bollock. And to be fair, I had just told a four year old, not to jump into a massive puddle. Even if everyone else did. Hmmm.

I ran down to the creek, but I was too late. Elliott saw me coming and he walked towards me looking like the 'monster from the lagoon'. It was more obvious that Elliott had been in the pool, because he had lighter skin than all the others. And he was covered in mud from head to foot. For a fleeting moment I thought about trying to clean him up before Jo saw him. But then I saw sense. A failed attempt to cover this up could only make things worse!

But I was always happy in my own mind that the boys in the village would look after Elliott. And there was a big part of me that was proud to see him doing the stuff that I did at his age. The other kids were a little older, five and six, and so they kind of took him under their wing. And he was fitting in like he was born there.

One morning I heard a scratching at the window. In the village this is what people do instead of knocking on the door. But it was six in the morning, so I knew it wouldn't be for me. In the early morning light I watched Elliott creep out of the door and disappear. I think it's because I was entirely at home again in the bush that I didn't think to stop him. It seemed the most natural thing in the world to me, for Elliot to go off with his mates to hunt for berries for breakfast. And I had no worries that Elliott would be frightened. In many ways I thought it would have been wrong not to let him go. And I made the mistake of putting that very point to Jo:

"It would have been wrong? It would have been wrong?! Oh for Christ's sake Stan, he's four years old! And you've let him wander off into the jungle with a bunch of five year olds."

Jo's mother's instincts were kicking in big time:

"There are snakes out there and God knows what. He could be in a swamp, up a tree ...." Jo put her head in her hands; not a good sign:

"What time did he go?"

I thought about lying. But Jo said, 'don't lie to me Stan' so that made it easier.

"Six o'clock?! Oh my God. He's been gone three hours. He could be dead!"

I made one final mistake, asking Jo if she fancied a cup of coffee. At which point, it was clearly the right time to wait for Elliott outside.

The minutes passed, and then the hours. It was after eleven now and no sign of the boys. The midday sun was getting hot, and I was starting to sweat. Maybe I had made the worst mistake of my life after all. I wandered around the village, and I saw two little kids playing marbles. Had they been into the bush that morning? No.

I had to keep a cool head. And decide when was the time to get help and go into the jungle to look for them. And then, just as I was starting to get really worried, in the distance, I could make out four figures. They were small boys emerging from the bush. They were moving very slowly, and I could see that the biggest one was carrying something on his shoulders. As they got closer, I could see that it was a little kid, and with my heart now racing I could soon see that it was Elliott.

I lifted him off the shoulder of his friend, and carried him inside. These were already great friends to my little boy. And the eldest calmly explained that Elliott had fallen asleep and so they took it in turns to carry him home.

♦

I'm so proud of Elliott. Not just of the way that he fits in with all the boys in the village, but of the way I know he is growing up into a fine young man.

On that first trip to PNG I took Jo and Elliott to a nearby dump, where people threw all their rubbish. There was a terrible smell in the midday heat, and you could see rats crawling all over the place. I just wanted them to see the worst bits of my homeland. There were little boys who lived there. And they were walking over broken glass and covered in flies, just looking for food. Elliott took it all in. He looked up at me and said:

"Dad, aren't we lucky?"

From that day, Elliott has never asked me for anything. And he always reminds me to take stuff over whenever I go home. He buys pencils and rubbers with his spending money, for me to take to his friends over there. He's no angel, but he's a good lad. And I'd give him my last penny, because I know that he'd give me his.

Elliot was so popular in the village, and there was still some novelty value for the locals, and so we never got a moment's privacy. That had always been the way for me since I'd left home, and Jo had experienced it too. But this year it was starting to wear her down a little bit, and also it was the first time that she had spent Christmas away from home. Maybe she still hadn't fully recovered from our reception in the good old US of A. So I thought it would be nice for us to stay in a hotel on Christmas day. Jo could have a nice bath, and we had a good day together, just the three of us.

Jo had been getting a bit tired of everyone coming up to us all the time. She's such a friendly girl, but she likes us to have our quiet time together when we can. And so for New Year I decided we should fly to a tiny island called Madang, which was renowned for being one of the most colourful islands in the South Pacific. And I assured Jo that they definitely didn't play rugby on the island so there was no way that anyone would know me.

We flew over on a little Cessna, and landed in a field within a few metres of the beach. This was paradise, and we could easily get lost here. Or so I thought. As we stepped off the plane, this tall guy came over to us beaming from ear to ear:

"Mr Gene, can I just say what a great honour it is for you to visit our hotel." Then he looked over his shoulder and yelled, *"Robert, he's here, he's here .... Get the champagne opened!"*

We were ushered to the hotel entrance, and wandered into the lobby to be met by six staff, all smiling and rushing forward to shake my hand. Someone said, 'yeah, it's Stanley Gene, for real.'

Jo just looked at me and shook her head.

It seemed that there wasn't actually anywhere in PNG where we could escape attention. I must say I thought it was quite funny, but for Jo's sake I kept trying to find somewhere quieter. We drove around the island, and managed to spend a whole day without coming across anyone at all. And then for New Year, we flew in the Cessna to an even smaller island, Karangat, which was about as big as Craven Park. It had a small two star hotel, and three boats. Perfect.

Karangat was very much a tourist place, not for how many people were there, it was just that there was nothing at all to do, other than sunbathe, eat, drink, and maybe do some fishing or diving. We concentrated on the first three for a couple of days, but then I had to have a go at my favourite hobby, fishing. I had worked on my technique a lot since the day I chucked my rod into the lake in East Park, so we got up early on New Years Eve to head for the shore. Either Jo was now fully chilled out, after a couple of days soaking up the sun, and wanted some more of the same. Or she had automatically reverted to 'mum' mode, because she didn't look at all happy as she surveyed the rickety little boat, manned by a grinning skipper who was smoking a spliff, sharpening a knife and sitting on a crate of beer:

"I don't like this Stan. You can't swim, Elliott can't swim and I'm not a good swimmer. Anything could happen out there."

I think she was probably thinking 'if the US government could kidnap us and hold us prisoner, then God knows what Bob Marley here with his big knife might do'. But after a few minutes of careful negotiation, Jo agreed that I could take Elliott out there, on the condition that Elliott had to suffer the humiliation of wearing two inflatable armbands. Thank God there wasn't another pair available.

So off we set, man and son into the great blue ocean, in the hands of a guy who looked like he really didn't know what he was doing, or care for that matter. But this was magnificent, it was a chance for me to show Elliott how a born hunter from the Pacific rainforest can stalk and kill his prey with awesome efficiency.

Two hours later and with eight empty beer cans rolling around the boat, we were getting a bit bored. And then, suddenly, Elliott fell off his seat, clinging on to his rod which had all but thrown him into the sea. The line was tight and twitching. He had a bite. Now I hadn't explained to Elliott that the one thing that can frighten me more than a snake ..... is a shark. And that is why I never learnt to swim. Bob and I looked at each other, clearly both expecting the other to help this small child battling with a monster of the sea. So we both did, and without any sign of awesome efficiency whatsoever, the three of us yanked a two foot tuna into the boat.

As we trooped into the hotel lobby, Elliott was grinning like a Cheshire cat. He could only just carry this fantastic fish, and couldn't wait to show his mum. Jo gave him a big hug and told him what a great fisherman he was, and he didn't stop smiling for an hour. The chef at the hotel promised Elliott that he'd cook it for our dinner, and so after we'd had a shower, we all came down for a drink and to wait for the feast that Elliott had provided.

The island was populated by a huge number of fruit bats, and during the day the coconut trees were covered by the bats while they were asleep. As night fell and the sky became darker, the fruit bats all woke up and started to flit around above our heads. It was so peaceful, watching the bats and listening to the sea, it was very easy to drift off. And when the chef arrived with a magnificent platter carrying our whole tuna, dressed with shrimps and leaves and fruit, he found that Elliott, who we had to thank for the meal, was asleep.

But Elliott didn't miss out. The chef wrapped his tuna in foil, and we could relive the whole adventure again the next day.

♦

It certainly had been the holiday of a lifetime in many ways, with some wonderful and some terrible memories, and we were all tired and ready to go home. That was, of course, after one more pig had bitten the dust to send us on our way.

Sydney airport was bustling, and reminded us immediately of what life was like outside the hidden world of New Guinea. Jo was looking forward to seeing her mum and dad, and I could see she was pleased to hear Stephanie's voice on the phone. I heard her say, 'hi mum, how are you?' and the usual catching up words, such as how much she was looking forward to a hot bath and her own bed. Elliott and I were looking out for our flight update on the big screens, but when I glanced back at Jo her face had dropped. And I wondered what had happened. She looked like someone had just whacked her in the face with a frying pan. What could possibly compare with being locked up in

Washington or losing Elliot in the jungle? Maybe we'd been burgled.

No such luck. It turned out that before we left Hull in mid December, we, or I, had forgotten to put the central heating on the timer. It had been off all the time. And during a particularly cold spell, an aluminium pipe in the loft had frozen and cracked. The water had broken out, with some force and the whole house was flooded. I started to wonder how much more Jo could take! But I didn't really want to find out.

So after a couple of nights at Hotel Paul and Stephanie, we moved into a little bed and breakfast just outside Beverley. It was very comfortable, with a real log fire, but we moved back home just as soon as we could.

♦

On the first day back at training, I knew I'd done the right thing signing for another two years. There was a real buzz about the place and I put that down to the influence of Tony Smith. Ok we had been relegated the year before, but we had shown a real fighting spirit, and played a lot of good footy. And as I said before, Tony was a massive influence on me.

I knew that I was becoming a better player. All my life I just wanted to get the ball and run. But Tony was influencing me to look at the little things in the game that made all the difference. I learnt how to use my fitness and reserve my energy, and to make sure that I always had the best chance of getting to the line. Tony always told me to concentrate on the small technical detail, but he never had a game plan for me. He often set tactical game plans for my team mates, but for me he simply said, 'just go on the field and do what you do.' He said he wanted to see me on the left and the right, all over the place, and the way he spent the time to give me confidence, he certainly got the best out of me. And in 2002 I scored twenty eight tries from twenty five games.

As a coach, Tony is incomparable. When he got the Great Britain position, anyone who knows anything in the game knew that he was the best man for the job. He's different to other top coaches because with the other guys there's always pressure. The way Tony is, he absorbs all the pressure himself, and he always seems to stay relaxed, and that takes the pressure off us. Sure, he can get angry, but I think any coach who does as much for his players as Tony does, has the right to blow a gasket when they let him down. And he's a funny guy who can take a joke. I always call him 'Long nose' on account of his long nose. Very childish I know, but it doesn't seem to piss him off.

And he's a really interesting guy. He was brought up in the country in Australia, and he's a very gifted horseman. When I first arrived at Huddersfield, he was renting a farmhouse that had a little airstrip in one of the fields. Tony had his pilots licence and he took me up in his landlord's plane from time to time.

His skill as a coach and a people manager seemed to have washed the painful memory of relegation clean from our minds. And we certainly didn't play like we had any negative thoughts. In fact we stormed the league winning all of our games. The only real rivals we had were Leigh, but we were much too strong for them, and there was never any doubt that we were going straight back to the Super League.

And Macca was there as Tony's lieutenant. He was the commander on the pitch, the club captain; he had a great brain and brilliant hands. But he had no pace at all. There was one match at Widnes that he was going so slow the fans thought he was cutting the grass. I hope to God that his son Ben has more pace. He's just started playing up in Hull for Skirlaugh under 9's team.

I enjoyed my footy tremendously that year, with a mandate to play in my own style, but with the added technical skill that made me a better player. The only games I didn't enjoy were against Hull K. R. Any player who plays against his home team will have some divided loyalties. But for me, it wasn't simply sentimentality, but a deep rooted knowledge that I owed a lot of my life to that club. And I will always be a crazy Rovers fan.

The worst game of all was in the Arriva Final between us and Rovers at Featherstone. I'd spoken to a lot of my mates in Hull before the match and they weren't too confident. But when the game started I was soon having a nightmare. In fact come to think of it I'd already had two stinkers that year against Rovers. But this was the worst of all, and midway through the second half, as a Rovers player made a break, I realised I was too late to get across and I ended up tripping him, and I was sent off.

I had been getting a lot of stick from a section of the Rovers fans, and as I walked off along the touchline, one of the Rovers supporters threw a full pint of beer in my face! Now I don't mind being booed. It usually means that those fans who are booing wished you were playing for them. You don't often hear a bad player getting booed by opposition fans. But this really pissed me off. I didn't see the guy's face, but I didn't want to get angry, because right behind him was my little boy and my missus. So I just licked my lips and said 'thanks mate' and walked off.

I think it's the fact that Jo and Elliott saw it all that really pissed me off. It didn't change the way I felt about the club in any way, but I did tell Neil Hudgell that if I could remember this guy's face and I saw him at the club I'd knock him out! I was so angry because the idiot had done it in front of my boy.

I don't think he'll come and say, 'sorry it was me', but if he does I guess I should buy him a pint.

♦

We finished the 2002 season with a win at Widnes, but we knew we were heading for the Super League long before that. It reinforced in my mind that this club should not have been relegated the year before. I couldn't think of many sides in the country that had a better coach and captain. And we had a stronger team as well, that had been improved by the addition of Brendan Costin, who was a truly excellent player. Paul Reilly, our full back, just had a brilliant season; he was as hard as nails but packed with ability. Paul is the hardest player I've ever played with, tougher even than Rob Wilson. For sure Rob was a madman, but pound for pound there was none harder than Paul. For any soccer fans reading this, it's kind of like comparing

Vinny Jones with Roy Keane. Although I can't really see Rob going to Hollywood.

The 2003 season quickly started to look like a springboard for the Giants. We were playing really well and holding our own with some style. We had a good win at home to St Helens, but the highlight for me was beating Wigan at the McAlpine Stadium. We absolutely walloped them and what made it sweeter for me, was that my PNG Kumuls captain, Adrian Lam, was playing for Wigan.

The press had built it up as a confrontation of two PNG stars, and I was pleased to get some coverage for our home country. After we had won I couldn't wait to speak to Adrian. But he didn't return my calls for a couple of weeks. I guess if it had been the other way around and he'd left similar messages for me, I'd have blanked him as well.

We had played virtually the whole season with most of the same team that had been promoted the year before, and it was quite a young squad. So when we finished seventh, we were justifiably proud of what we had achieved. A lot of it was down to the coaching. We were always well prepared and every player knew what he had to do to bring success to the club.

Tony wanted to take the club to the next level. Seventh in the Super League was the highest position the Giants had ever reached, and it was clear that cash was needed to bolster up the squad if we were going to break into the top six. But the cash wasn't on the table, so when Tony was asked to consider the coaching job at Leeds, after Daryl Powell had left, he went. With the resources that were available, he thought that he had taken Huddersfield as far as he could.

I was sorry to see Tony go. We had previously talked about me going with him, if and when he ever left Huddersfield, but that was not on the cards. Daryl Powell had made some signings before he left and spaces in the first team were too tight.

So when the new coach at Huddersfield, Jon Sharp, talked to me about extending my contract for a further three years, I was happy to sign. I was certainly at home with the Giants, and Jo and I were looking for a house in the area.

I was playing well and the team was on the up. And I felt well and truly settled. So why move?

8

Mum's the Word

1986 - 1991
Goroka

Even at the age of eleven, you can lay awake at night worrying about things. Usually things that have already passed and you can't do anything about. But when it's as important as the future of your education, and whether you'll have one or not, then something's not quite right. To decide whether kids should continue to go to school, on the strength of an exam taken at the age of eleven surely has to be wrong. Kids at eleven should be worried whether they're going to make the footy team, or why their dick grows when they see a pig, not whether they're going to spend their lives doing what they're ancestors did, if they couldn't remember their five times table on one particular day.

But that's exactly what happened. On the day the results were posted, there were kids walking away from school for the last time with no hope of a second chance. Over here in the UK there are later chances in life if you miss out the first time. Even after you have left school you can do things like 'Learn Direct', and there are all sorts of courses you can do through the Open University. There are so many chances to learn things, just by watching telly or going onto the internet. I take that for granted now. But back home, if you screw up before you sprout your first pubic hair, you will be picking coffee until the day you die.

I've seen the effects of the system. I know guys who I was at primary school with, just falling away with no hope of recovering. It's just not right. There are guys in their early twenties sitting around the house all day, because they have nothing else to do. And they never really had a choice, because the school system never gave them a chance.

Even the kids who made it through the sixth grade had no guarantee of a job. They could fall away at eleventh grade and still have no chance of work. And I've seen guys who do get work but just don't know how to adapt. One of the things I love about this country is that kids get the opportunity to do work experience while they are at school. They get two weeks working in an office, and finding out what it's like in the job world. What a great idea. I hope they appreciate that.

◆

Thank God I'd done well enough to get my place in Goroka High School. If I had passed, but not so well, I would have ended up in a school twenty miles away, so I was well pleased, and still thanking Mr Harris. Even so, it meant getting up an hour earlier, because the high school was on the other side of the airport, which was nearly an hour away on foot. As the crow flies it's less than twenty minutes, but we had to walk all the way around the airport.

The long walk was compensated though by the fact that we now had a uniform. It was a bright yellow t-shirt and blue shorts. I loved it. We didn't have a uniform at primary school and so this was very special. I was very proud of my uniform but it also made me feel a bit self conscious.

Sometimes we used to catch a bus, which took us right round the airport to the school. It was a rickety old thing, with seats down either side. Quite often there were no seats left when I got on, so I had to stand in the middle hanging on to the rail. When I was standing up in the bus I felt like everyone was looking at me and I was getting really embarrassed. So after a few days, I put another t-shirt in my school bag. And when I came out of school, I took my yellow t-shirt off and put my other one on before I got on the bus. I don't really know why I did this. The other boys did it too. On the one hand I loved my uniform, but it seemed like for some reason I didn't want everyone to see it. It was a bit daft when I think about it because the bus always stopped when it saw a yellow uniform. There are no bus stops like we have over here, so we'd have to run along and wave when the bus arrived. So if we weren't wearing our yellow tops, the bus didn't stop! I learnt to swap t-shirts pretty quickly.

Sometimes I used to walk all the way to school with Tony and Lulu. We were all as excited as each other with our new school. And we often talked about the primary school, and how great it was to be the first year to pass through the school. We all decided that we wanted to be primary school teachers, partly because it was such an important job, but we also wanted to be Mr Harris. He was a god.

Lulu was getting more serious about himself now. And he decided that this was the right time to change his name to Keith. He thought that would obviously get him more respect. But we just took the piss out of him endlessly, and we told everyone we could that he was actually called Lulu. I still do, every time I go to visit him at his work in Port Moresby. There's something really funny about someone trying to appear more grown up.

But we had to learn quickly. School was now so different to our days at primary school. We had never really been to the city and had just enjoyed life in our village. We didn't know what to expect - more sums, reading and singing? The whole thing was a real eye opener; we'd walk to and from school and see a lot of cars on the roads, and the school itself was massive. It had rows of classrooms, a gym and God knows how many sceptic toilets. It was funny really because it was just Goroka, but at the same time it seemed like another world.

And lessons too were different. No more bringing in the biggest mango we could find for our homework! In the seventh grade the core subjects were mathematics, English, social science, science and sports. We also had practical skills, which the boys did, and home economics for the girls. The practical skills were stuff like carpentry and carving. And the home economics were basically cooking, with some domestic work and cleaning thrown in. I think they realised that it was not all that politically correct, and so the girls can do practical skills as well now. And the boys can do cooking.

We also did a lot of agricultural studies, which involved coffee growing, livestock and land care. As well as that we did some studies called commerce. And at the end of the eighth grade we had to choose between the two options; agriculture or commerce. If you chose commerce, then you were aiming for a job in the city; it covered all aspects of different types of work including health, shipping and finance. The agriculture option was the equivalent for guys wanting to be able to work the land. This option was very comprehensive and taught us a lot about the tradition of our country.

This choice of options meant that in the ninth grade you would go into either a business school, or an agriculture school; and that became the core of your study. Coming from the village I always loved playing on the land, and so I chose agriculture, and it was great. In the mornings we finished our indoor studies, and in the afternoon, after we had changed into working clothes, we went outside.

The agriculture course was really practical. We kept chickens, and grew bananas and cabbages. And we learnt all about insects and how to protect our crops. We ploughed the land ourselves and then each of us in the class planted our own cabbage. Once it had grown, the teacher gave every one of us a mark, and that went towards the end of year school report.

The school made money out of the agriculture classes by selling the bananas and vegetables to the hotel and at the markets, so we were getting real practical guidance on how to become self sufficient.

This money supplemented the school fees, which were three hundred Kinas a year when I first arrived. As I said before I am so grateful that my family paid me through school. Three hundred Kinas was a lot of money to my folks, and it was at a time when they didn't have much. Kaula had just retired from his job at the hospital and so at first, all the money that came in was from anything we could sell that we'd grown, and that I hadn't given to Mr Harris! So Auntie Christina still carried on paying my fees.

And the fees just kept going up. In the eighth grade they were five hundred kinas, but they were about to get even more expensive for me.

I was doing okay at school for sure, but for some reason, my mum and dad got the idea that I needed to concentrate more on my studies. I don't know to this day if the teachers had said anything to them …. I thought I was doing fine. For sure, it was all new to me, and I was proud that I had gone further than anyone in my family before me, but I didn't know what to expect. Tony and Lulu had older brothers who had been to the high school before them, and so they knew a lot more about it than I did.

Anyway, at the point that I had taken my agriculture option Mum, Dad and Christina decided that I should start boarding at the school. And I always thought that they liked me! But their minds were made up that it would be best for me in the long term. So for the ninth and tenth grade that was it. I was at boarding school, just a ten minute sprint across the airport.

♦

In all honesty, I don't think I was really cut out for boarding. I was always dying to get home, because I was used to being the kid in the village, and messing about with my mates. But I guess, at the age of fourteen those days were over for me.

And it was so boring living at school. There was nothing to do outside study hours, and I think I was starting to get on everybody's nerves. So the headmaster gave me a job. And it was a top job - looking after the chickens. That was great fun and I started to enjoy my time a lot more. In the mornings I'd get up and feed them, and at night I'd go out, armed with a torch and a broom to look for rats. The really big ones used to come to steal the chickens' eggs. It was like a fairground game, jumping about in among the squawking chickens, trying to smash the brains out of any rat that scuttled by, with my big broom. I was having a great laugh and the long nights soon started to fly!

Sometimes we had an order from a hotel, and so I'd get up early to kill and chop the chickens ready for them to be picked up. I suppose when I said 'looking after' the chickens they probably wouldn't agree, as it seemed to encompass either stomping around looking for rats, or simply killing them. And I have to admit; when we had an order it was time to celebrate.

We all knew that there was a party coming when we had a chicken order, because we got to keep the necks and the wings. And on the Saturday night I could prepare a great meal. We didn't have any pans so we used an old oil tin, and we dropped the chicken necks in with some cabbage and made a big stew. It was brilliant, because we had all the ingredients we needed in the school garden - chilli, ginger, all sorts. All the kids who were boarding had a feast. It was always the best time of the week.

Every other weekend we got to go home to see our families. It seems strange now, but to me it was like travelling around the world, rather than round the airport. Even though the village was only forty minutes away, it might as well have been four days, because they were two entirely separate worlds.

I looked forward to seeing Maul and going out hunting with Kaula, and it was always great to be home again.

So if we were lucky enough to have a chicken order on the opposite weekend to home visit, life was sweet.

♦

It was at the end of the ninth grade that I first started taking an interest in rugby. Up until then I had just played soccer, apart from jacket fighting and nut shooting of course. I had played a little bit of touch rugby in the village, but my interest was definitely ignited when Lulu came back from a rugby tour he had been on to Australia.

Lulu had played rugby with his older brothers from quite a young age, and he soon became a pretty good player. He was tough enough. I'm sure that was partly because he had such a crap name, and he had to be! But he obviously had a lot of skill too because he was chosen to play for the PNG schools under-60kg team.

The representative teams at school level in New Guinea were always done by weight rather than age. It makes for a more balanced team and match. If you do it by age, sometimes you'll get a big hairy fifteen year old playing alongside a shrimp. Also we'd never win a game against the Samoans because they're all so huge.

And so the flip side, of course, is that you have an under-60kg team with an age range from twelve to eighteen. But I think if you organised teams like that in the UK it wouldn't work. You would find some of the players in the under-60kg team carrying Power Rangers, and others with a pocket full of condoms. Pre-match team talks would be a nightmare ..... 'Come on lads, let's kick some fuckin' ass!' ...... 'Has anyone seen my Transformer?' .... 'Screw your Transformer, this is serious' ...... 'Cowabunga!' ...... 'Oh Christ!'

But it seemed to work okay in PNG, so Lulu (or Keith) had his chance to shine among this collection of physiological freaks that set out for Australia. And it was Lulu's amazing experience that really clicked for me. He came back with a load of photographs and his stories about flying. It was totally beyond my imagination to be on an aeroplane and take off up into the sky. And he was completely knocked out by the country he had visited, and full of tales, right down to what he had to eat. He was telling me about the barbeques, the steaks and the beaches and it was at that point that I had a life changing realisation:

'Okay then, I'll play rugby.'

I really thought that it was a way to see the world, although I'd never played a proper game in my life, and so there was no guarantee it would work for me. But if Lulu could do it, why couldn't I?

So it was in 1989 that I actually started playing rugby. For those of you that are still struggling to guess my age, I was somewhere between thirteen and seventeen!

1989 was a life changing year for me in two ways. The first is that I grew a love for the game that would ultimately give me my livelihood, take me around the world, and find me a new life and everything that comes with it. Everything that comes with it is a wonderful wife and partner, two fantastic boys, some great friends. As well as that it has grown me as a man; given me confidence, assurance and even taught me how to gain security for my family. So what could be bigger than that?

In the long term, and with the benefit of hindsight, nothing can really rank as a more important change than that. But as a thirteen to seventeen-year-old, who has never been more than forty minutes away from his home, some events are earth shattering when they happen.

Life had always been simple for me. I had everything that I needed to grow up happily, a home and plenty of food. Okay I didn't have many clothes, and my trainers had holes that a tarantula could sneak through. But I had a mum and dad who did everything they could in their power to see that I was alright. Maul made sure I was clean when I went to school and looked after me when I had fever, and did all those things a mum does that you don't really notice. And Kaula never once said to me, 'no Son, I'm too busy.' Whether it was taking me hunting, or to the market, or scooping worms out of trees, no matter how knackered he was, he always had time for me. He was the perfect dad.

And all the villagers in Segu gave support to each other. There was a real family community, the type that I hear old people in the UK say they had fifty years ago. In particular, of course, I had Auntie Christina who had kept a close eye on me, and had given a lot in terms of both money and encouragement to get me through school.

Soon after Kaula retired we moved. We didn't go far, just about five minutes away to a settlement called Genoka. I guess you would call it a ghetto. There were about a hundred or so huts, all close together. And there was a bit more happening than in the village. Kaula's second wife had a house quite near. But that didn't make any difference to any of us. I didn't know her at all, and it was a part of Kaula's life that was kept entirely separate from our family. It seems a bit strange talking like that, now that I have lived in the UK for over a decade. But that's how it is back home. Anyway, believe it or not Kaula hadn't stopped there! He still had time to take a third wife in his later years. It didn't make any difference to me. He has always been a loving husband and a special dad, and I wouldn't have wanted him to be any other way.

The reason we moved was that Kaula had invested his retirement money in a little house that was also a shop. As well as working the land, we could make some money selling fruit, vegetables, rice, oil, sugar and general household stuff. Kaula didn't want to just retire and sit around the house. He always wanted to do everything he could for his family.

It was a small house, but big enough for the four of us; Kaula, Maul, me and my sister Judy. Oh yes, Judy. I haven't talked about my sister so far, not because we don't get on or any other particular reason. I guess that I spent so many of my early years playing in shit and eating worms that my lifestyle probably didn't appeal to a teenage girl! But believe me; Judy has had a big part to play in my life and never once let me feel that I was an only child.

Also Judy was six years older than me, so the chances of us having any mutual interests were zero. Unless of course girls had been allowed to play rugby, then we could have ended up on the same under-50kg team!

And I didn't see much of Judy after we had moved to the settlement. For one thing I was at school, but also she had just got a good job in Goroka. She was the pay mistress at a big shop called Stimpsons and so when I was at school we saw each other now and then at the weekends, or, in the evening before I started boarding.

But we did have a normal brother-sister relationship. That is to say I regularly pissed her off, and she equally regularly complained to Mum about me. It never occurred to me at the time, but now I come to think about it, she did say some weird things in the heat of an argument like, 'why don't you get back to your mum?' or 'go back to the village where you belong.' For a start, I never went running to Mum if I was in a row, and secondly, I belonged here. But I guess women are sometimes hard to figure out when you're older, let alone when you're still in short pants. I know that now, but at the time I just thought Judy was crap at arguing and had lost her thread!

It still never worried me even when Maul joined in with the cryptic comments. Now and then, when Judy was moaning about something I had done, Maul would say, 'well Judy, it was you that wanted us to have Stanley in the first place.' Kaula would just smile and shake his head. For sure we were a close family, but I started to wonder if Judy was somehow involved in my conception. We didn't do any sex education at school so you can understand my confusion. The only bit I understood, I had learnt by looking after the chickens, before I killed them of course.

And then one Sunday it all came spectacularly to a head. A lot of our arguments were caused by the tiniest of incidents, like me dropping Judy's dress into the fire; well they were tiny to me. And on this occasion it was no different. In fact I can't actually remember what sparked the row; I know that's often the case when you're a bloke. Maybe I'd dropped some fried worms on Judy's bed while I was looking for my footy and rushing to eat my breakfast at the same time. It was more likely the fact that I'd pinched some rice off a plate, which Judy was preparing for dinner. While something so terrible might prompt the American government to deploy a team of weapons inspectors or at the very least, arrest me, Judy was cooler than that. Or so I thought.

I had been playing footy with Robin and a couple of other guys, and the sun was getting really hot, so we had decided to pack it in. I knew that Kaula and Maul would be back from church by now and it would nearly be time for some food. And I was dying of thirst, so I made my way home.

As I got near to the settlement I could hear some terrible shouting. And it was coming from our house. Aha, it was Judy having her weekly explosion. I wondered what it was all about this time, but I didn't have to wonder for too long. As I stuck my head around the door, Judy fixed her eyes on me like a viper that was about to strike. Or at the very least like a pig that I had just swished at with a baseball bat and missed. Either way I nearly crapped in my pants. Fair enough, Judy was a girl, but she could be ferocious, and I knew this look only appeared when the shit was about to hit a wind farm.

What actually hit me was a pair of my pants, right between the eyes. Maul was sat by the fire stirring something, and Kaula was making 'calm down' kind of signs, a bit like the bloke who had to tell Hitler that the Italians had swapped sides. But Judy was not to be calmed down:

"No Dad, I've had enough! He's finally done it, the little idiot, and I'm not putting up with it a second longer!" she screamed as she stuffed my clothes into a suitcase.

Now that in itself wasn't such a big deal. Firstly Judy had tried to pack me on my way at least twenty times before. And secondly, I didn't have all that many clothes, so it wouldn't take me too long to unpack. What really spooked me though, was that frightening look in her eyes, coupled with a threat that I hadn't heard before, 'either he goes or I go'. This time she really meant business, and she yelled:

"Now piss off Stanley. Go and live in the village with your mum!"

And with that she hurled my hastily packed leaving luggage out of the house. Over the past year or so Judy had been doing this more regularly, and also it occurred to me that once or twice she had called Christina my Mum. Maul always said, 'naaah, don't be silly, Christina's your auntie' so, as ever, that was enough to satisfy me.

On this occasion, as luck would have it, at the very moment that the suitcase flew through the door, my Uncle Dixon was arriving for dinner with Auntie Christina. They came round every Sunday after church. Anyway, the case hit Uncle Dixon on the head and then fell half opened to the floor, spilling three socks and a catapult. But what happened next made my jaw drop to my feet.

While Uncle Dixon got to his feet and rubbed his head, Christina looked at Maul and said:

"Okay I'll take the suitcase. Judy's said it now, we all heard it. Stanley can come home with me."

I looked at Judy, and Judy looked at the wall. Maul was crying her eyes out so I looked at Kaula. And he gently nodded at me. It turned out that everybody knew the truth apart from me.

At first I didn't believe it. How could this be true? But no one looked like they were about to burst out laughing and shout 'Gotcha!' so I didn't know what to think. I became really angry, but as I looked around at everyone, the truth became clearer in their expressions that showed sadness, guilt and in Uncle Dixon's case, a look that said 'well you've done it now'.

I am Christina's son.

How come everybody knew about this all along and no one had told me? To give her credit, Judy had tried a few times, but hadn't raised a spark! I had been brought up by Maul and Kaula, my Mum and Dad, and that's all I ever knew. Sure, Christina had paid a lot of money to get me through school, but she was Kaula's brother, so as far as I was concerned, of course she was my auntie. And if Kaula was my dad, then there's no way that Christina could be my mum. Sometimes I'm a bit slow on the uptake and Judy had to explain that one to me later.

So Kaula wasn't my dad either? Oh God, this get's worse. And everybody knew about it all along. I grabbed Dixon's arm:

"Did you know Uncle Dixon?"

Of course Uncle Dixon did know, but I was relieved to confirm that he wasn't my dad either.

It's one of the strangest things imaginable, that you find out that everything you thought your world was built on wasn't actually what you thought. And that quite a lot of people knew this all along. It makes you feel like a bit of a dick; but an angry one.

And then, with all the composure of someone who had just had a recipe book returned, Christina looked at me and said:

"Okay Stanley, let's go home."

I was so mad and shocked that I just followed.

Christina took hold of my suitcase and we walked the five minutes back to the village, followed by Uncle Dixon who was carrying my mattress on his back. We went into Christina's house and all sat down. Well that was it. In the morning I had woken up with a mum, a dad and a big sister. And by the afternoon I had a different mum, no dad and a little brother. That had been quite a day.

By nightfall I still couldn't really get my head around it. As I settled down on my mattress, I listened to the constant hum of the insects in the jungle, and wondered what on earth was going to happen to me next.

♦

My first afternoon at Christina's house had been a quiet one. But unbeknown to me, down at the settlement things had been anything but tranquil. Kaula had spent most of the afternoon trying to keep Maul calm:

"Stanley's fifteen now, he has to know the truth, and he is old enough to make up his own mind."

Maul didn't see it like that, and she let Kaula know, in no uncertain terms:

"He's old enough to make up his own mind? What do you know? You're an old man and you don't know how to make up your own mind!"

That was a bit harsh. Maybe Maul was having a little dig at Kaula's marital arrangements, but it's more likely that she was just hitting out in despair:

"I've brought Stanley up ever since he was a tiny baby. Looked after him, cared for him and I have always loved him as my son. Where has Christina been? What has she been doing all this time?"

"Well ..... she has paid all Stanley's school fees." Shut up Kaula.

Maul glared at him, like a lioness that has seen one of her cubs stolen from her. Kaula took the hint and let Maul carry on:

"We have always provided for Stanley from the very first day, he has never wanted for anything. Christina can't take him away."

And Maul was right of course. I know that she fed me from the very first day that she became my mother. Every day for month after month she gave me sweet potato juice and the mashed up potato. These are the things that give you a healthy start in life and I had always felt secure. In fact, that is something that I have brought to the UK. Ever since Leo was born two years ago we have given him mashed sweet potato and juice. He loves it, and I love watching him eat it. These things that are passed down from generation to generation often form the basis for the strength of a family. We can learn so much from our parents, even though they aren't always entirely rational.

Maul had stormed out of the house; Judy had already disappeared somewhere, so Kaula finally had a bit of peace and quiet. And then after a few moments it occurred to him that Maul was not in the best frame of mind, so he decided to go and look for her. He wearily pulled himself out of his chair and went outside.

He didn't have to look too far. Maul had spent the last five minutes breaking a branch off a nearby coffee tree and was striding off up the track. The branch was about four foot long, and Kaula wondered what Maul was planning to use it for. So he asked, and got the reply he had feared:

"I'm going to give Christina a piece of my mind. And show her that she can't just run around taking my kids away."

She was actually going to give Christina a piece of the branch, and a damn good beating! Maul was an old woman, and this would have been funny if it wasn't my family. Thankfully Kaula managed to persuade her that 'it wasn't in Stanley's best interests for his old mum to smash his new mum's brains out with a branch'. And all credit to Kaula, who in doing so was actually taking his own life in his hands! But I guess when all is said and done, Maul and Kaula had been a loving husband and wife for many years, and the truth is, that Maul was the last person in the world that would ever want to hurt Kaula.

When I woke up the next morning I still didn't feel right. I still had the instinct that Maul and Kaula were my mum and dad. They had been for fifteen years and that wouldn't just go away in a day. I went to school with the weight of the world on my shoulders. Christina packed me off and told me to come home at teatime. She had already decided that I no longer needed to board and that I should come home every night, so I did.

I didn't really concentrate on my studies that day. I wasn't even interested in the agriculture work in the afternoon. And I went home to see if everything I thought had happened the day before actually had. I arrived at Christina's just as she was returning from work.

But all my things had gone. My mattress and suitcase, and all the clothes that I had unpacked were nowhere to be seen. Maul and Kaula had been up to the village during the day, and taken my stuff back to the settlement. Christina sat down on the floor next to me. She had a mother's love for her son, and understood more about me than I did myself:

"Don't worry Stanley, you go back."

I often wonder why Christina, my mum, told me to go back to Maul and Kaula again. When I think about it, and what I know now about Christina's life, it's just another example of her incredible strength. I can remember her saying to me years later, 'whatever you do, I'm still young and I'm still working. You have to look after Maul and Kaula.' And that sums up my mum more than anything. Believe it or not, to this day, I have never actually asked Christina if she is my real mum. The words have never left my mouth. But I know.

Christina was right. I belonged with Maul and Kaula, and Judy. Nothing was any different other than I was now learning who I was. But that happens to us all, as we go through life. And when I got back to the house in the settlement, it was as if nothing had changed. My mattress was back in its place, Maul was cooking and Kaula was smiling at me. I was pleased to be home:

"What's that big branch doing outside the door?" I asked.

Maul carried on cooking, and Kaula's smile spread a bit, until Maul caught his eye and it disappeared. They still kept a bit of pretence up for a while saying that Judy had 'lost her marbles' but I think they were just trying to protect my feelings.

But in a strange way I soon came to accept the whole situation and I was actually quite pleased. Everything was out in the open and we could all get on with our lives. The following weekend the whole village got together for a meeting, and it was agreed that 'enough was enough'. It was almost as if I wasn't there, and it turned out that virtually everybody had known who I was before I did! Presumably Uncle Dixon had told them. It all made me feel a bit of an arse again, but as it had all been accepted by everyone else, then that was fine by me.

So now I had two mums and a dad. Maul and Kaula were actually my auntie and uncle now, but our relationship never changed, they would always be Mum and Dad. But Christina too was my mum, and in a lot of ways it was great to have three parents looking out for me. Judy was still Judy and I also had a little brother. Ben was now five, I always thought he was my cousin, and he often came to stay with me. But now it was brilliant to have my own little brother.

And I never asked Christina who my dad was or Ben's for that matter. I wasn't ready for that, and it wasn't my place to ask the question. And to be honest, I wasn't at all bothered. Christina would tell me when she was ready. In fact, at the time Christina was carrying a baby, and soon enough I would have another brother or sister. So there was plenty to occupy us all without any more complications. Maybe that was one for the future. But at that very moment, I felt as happy as I had always done.

♦

I was playing more and more rugby, and it was becoming an obsession for me. I was no longer playing soccer, and soon I made it to the school team. When I wasn't at school or playing for the school, I played rugby with the boys in the village.

All I wanted to do was play rugby, and while Lulu and Tony were getting ready to go off to college, nothing could have been further from my mind. Christina was now being more open when she talked to me, and so wasn't shy to give me a bollocking. Sometimes having two mums isn't such a breeze! She was determined that I would become a teacher and kept on at me to finish my studies as well as I could.

But I didn't hear her. All I heard was the guys in the village saying how good I was going to be at Rugby, and I was playing for the village team or practicing almost every hour I had to myself. Even Kaula had a quiet word with me. He had always told me to do what makes me happy, but he knew that I was a bright lad and I couldn't spend all my life just playing footy. That was very true, but I was only sixteen, and so the importance of that advice was entirely lost on me.

I never got into any trouble at school, but in the last few months I started to miss a few lessons, usually because I was playing footy. And when the exams came around, I have to say, in teacher's language, that I did not fulfil my potential. Maybe if I'd put as much effort into my studies as I had into my rugby then I would have got better results. And I almost certainly would have followed a different career, so I wouldn't be where I am now. I'm not suggesting that kids shouldn't take their schooling seriously, but someone was looking out for me.

When the exams started, I just hadn't studied enough and I remember a teacher telling me that the worst time to study is just before the exam. Now that presented a question in itself. Was there any point in studying at the last minute to try to salvage a result? I decided to go with the flow. So much so that on one day as I arrived at school I was surprised to find out that there was an exam.

So you'll be surprised to hear I didn't get the top grades. And I have to say, that while it didn't get me a round of applause at home, I am now eternally grateful.

Rugby wasn't my only distraction. At around the time of my tenth grade I started to hang around with a bunch of lads from the settlement. Well, in a funny sort of way, they were hanging around me, because I was so good at footy, it was cool to be my mate. But these lads were not the types that my parents wanted me to be with. They were known as 'Rascals' and they caused a lot of trouble.

They started with a bit of shoplifting and smoking marijuana. There was a never ending supply of marijuana in PNG; it just grew like weeds. So there was never a market for selling it, because it was so easy to find. I didn't know it at first but the Rascals were soon graduating to more serious crime. They had started breaking and entering, and stealing cars. The worst I had done so far was stealing chocolates and stuff. If I had thought that the shopkeeper was trying to make a living, just like Kaula, I wouldn't have done it. But I wasn't in the thick of it, although these guys were my mates, I wasn't around all the time. Some of them played footy, but not as often as me. And I also liked going up to the village at the weekends to see Christina and Ben and do some work on the land.

So I had other interests, but I was close enough to the Rascals to get sucked into the trouble. And as things were getting more hairy, there were three episodes that happened that convinced me that ultimately, this wouldn't be the life for me.

The first was on a hot night at the settlement. We had all gathered outside a six-to-six club, what we would call a night club in the UK. We sat outside, looking through the windows, watching people getting drunk and dancing. The plan was to ambush a car, and we waited until our victim staggered out into the moonlight. As he reached his car we unleashed a hail of rocks, thrown or launched from slingshots, and his car was trashed in seconds. The guy, floundering around, without a clue what was happening as his windows smashed one by one, didn't look at all funny to me. At that moment I kind of wondered what exactly was the point.

But the Rascals weren't particularly clever criminals and they came up with some hair brained schemes. One night, we had planned to break into a shop. Rather than take the obvious route of smashing a window, one bright spark decided that pouring boiling water onto it would break it more quietly. So instead of a quick 'smash and grab' three Rascals carried an oil drum full of boiled water up to the shop window. Their grunts of effort, and yelps as their hands burnt, probably attracted more attention than the sound of breaking glass. But I was fascinated to see what would happen. It worked, and the lads got in. But I was more interested in how the crack spread across the glass as it steamed up, and as soon as it collapsed I ran off.

But I really decided that a life of petty crime was not for me when Uncle Dixon heard somewhere that I had been seen stealing chocolate or something. He beat the living daylights out of me. And just like Mr Christopher's length of hose had done, all those years ago, with that family act of an extremely painful beating, Dixon had set me on the right road again. I was aching for a couple of days, but happily able to play footy again by the weekend. That was the first time that I realised I could recover quickly from injury, something that has helped me throughout my career!

As I always say, I have never regretted anything I have done in my life. It all goes to make the man I am today. And the Rascals weren't just a bunch of losers. They were my friends for a time. I got trainers, rugby boots and shorts from them, so it would be wrong of me to just put them down. I know it wasn't right, but sometimes life can be very tough. And I thank God that I was given a gift that later opened so many doors for me.

◆

My direction was getting clearer and clearer to me. I just loved playing footy all the time. Our village team kept on winning, and that was all I wanted to do. So when I say my direction was getting clearer, I should say I knew where I wanted to get to in life, but in all honesty I didn't know how to get there.

And my step up to playing rugby at a formal level came from the most unexpected source. Crime levels in Goroka, and PNG as a whole were on the increase. Alcohol and drug related crimes were becoming more and more common, and the police were thinking of ways of stemming the tide. Does that sound familiar? Thankfully, no one came up with anti-social behaviour orders as a solution. In PNG anti-social behaviour could be forgetting to invite your uncle round for dinner on Sunday, or letting your pig watch someone having a crap. Vandalism, assault and theft are crimes. It's quite simple.

But nevertheless, keeping a handle on crime in a third world country is difficult. But the initiative that the police force in Goroka came up with was brilliant and an absolute godsend for me. They started up a police rugby club and team called the Royals. And in 1991, the team was going to start playing in the Goroka league. But rather than just filling the team with their own recruits, the force went out and about finding the best players from the villages and settlements around the area.

Not only that, but they provided training and facilities for anyone who wanted to play footy. At first the Rascals thought that the police were just setting a trap for them. That they would go up to the training ground and all get arrested. But I was picked out to play with the squad, and that is when things really started to happen for me.

And the police used me to get to the Rascals. I was sure that there was no trap, and so I persuaded a lot of the guys to come up and play at the training ground. And from then on there was a change in the relationship between the police and the community, including the Rascals.

When the team was formed even the Police Commissioner and his assistant came down to see what was happening. It was great for the police and great for the government. Because sure enough, within weeks of the Royals being formed, the crime rate around Goroka started to fall. Before the rugby team started, if there had been a breaking and entering, the police would struggle to solve the crime because no one in the community would help them. Now if there was a B and E, they would have thirty or forty informants.

When people in the UK come up with initiatives to reduce crime through sport I think we should take it seriously. The Rascals were committing crimes because they had nothing else to do. Now the Police Commissioner could come down to the training ground and see the police and Rascals getting closer, sharing a beer or a cigarette. It had worked like a dream.

And now I was getting proper kit. The police bought me boots and shorts and I really felt like I was getting somewhere. Kaula could see that I was excited, but he kept telling me not to get too carried away.

And we also got lunches provided. The best four or five of us, who were going to make the team, even went to eat with the police in their canteen.

The guy who had come up with the idea was called Joe Bulhage, a national intelligence officer for the police. I guess he was just doing his job, brilliantly well, but I can honestly say that he was the first major influence on my rugby career. I still go to see him now whenever I'm back in PNG. Joe to policing was like Mr Harris was to teaching – a genius. He was very forward thinking and wasn't afraid to try something new to solve an old problem. And he had the brains to see that rugby is like a religion in PNG, and how that could help him.

He's retired now and a couple of years ago he stood for the national elections as speaker. I supported his campaign, and he nearly made it, coming second. The guy that won the election knew that Joe could have beaten him, so he employed him as his bodyguard and media officer. That's the sort of combination you wouldn't see over here, apart from maybe Alastair Campbell, but Joe has everything he needs to be good at both.

I have absolutely no doubt that the police team changed everything for me. It took me on at a time when I had drifted out of school, and I had been involved with the Rascals. I loved playing rugby, and while I had known that Lulu had been to Australia through playing the sport, I didn't actually have a plan to take myself anywhere at all.

And it is so often the case in life that something happens to you, that is entirely out of your control, which tells you where you are going to go next. I know that I couldn't cope in PNG now, certainly not in the city, there's still too much crime. I could survive in the village, living off the land.

But thanks to Joe Bulhage I don't have to.

9

Blackberries

2004 – 2005
Huddersfield

There are always certain teams that always seem to be bouncing up and down. They're not quite good enough for the Super League, but that bit too good for the National league. It must be a nightmare for the fans – one year watching their team smashing everyone out of sight, and the next season struggling all year to get enough points to survive. I guess it's never dull but it can't be good for the nerves.

Its fair to say that Huddersfield had been one of those teams in the past. But for the last two or three years, there were signs that the club was climbing the stairs. With Tony Smith in charge there had been a confidence about the place, and everybody believed in the ability of the team. We had done well in 2003, finishing comfortably in the middle of the table, but when Tony left, I wondered whether the progress would carry on, or whether we'd start to bounce around again.

I know that some of the fans were saying that the club couldn't match Tony's ambition, and so that was why he had gone to Leeds. But the one thing that Tony had left was a settled squad, who had improved together and I for one was proud of what we had achieved. Sure enough, Tony wanted money to buy players, but any coach worth his salt is always trying to bring in better players. The fans, and I'm sure even the board, would start to worry if the coach said everything was alright and there was no need to improve the squad!

To be fair we still had some very good players in the team. Of course Paul Reilly was still there, along with Chris Thorman, Jimmy Evans and Chris Nero. They were all great players, and there was no doubt that with the wind behind us we could have another good year.

But Jon Sharp had a difficult act to follow. Tony was a class above any coach I had worked with, and a lot of our success was down to him. Nobody at the club wanted to start bouncing again and so there was a lot of weight on Jon's shoulders when he took the job. In his favour, the team hadn't changed much at all, and we all knew each others game. Also, coming from his job as assistant coach at St Helens, he had a very strong pedigree.

And he had a fantastic chairman behind him as well. I always think, just like with Neil Hudgell at Hull KR, it's so important that the chairman is a rugby man and loves the club. And Ken Davy is Mr Huddersfield; he's absolutely crazy about the club. God knows how much money he's put in over the years, but they certainly wouldn't be where they are now without him. He was good to me as well and treated me like a friend.

I remember just before the 2004 season, the club were getting worried because I hadn't got back from Goroka. I was at home in the village and the phone rang. Ben had picked it up and was speaking pidgin and then he shouted me over and said:

"Stanley, there's a white man calling from England and he says he's your boss, but he thinks you're called Jean!"

It was Ken asking when I was planning to come back to Huddersfield. I'd said that I was coming back and the club knew that and I had signed the contract. But I'd just lost track of the time. I'd already had a call from Macca telling me the club were worried and asking where I was, so I kind of expected a call.

But Ken is the type of guy that would just ring me to say hello and I'd count him as a friend. I'm really pleased for him now and he deserves any success he has.

So when pre-season training started, there was a lot of anticipation about the place. We had a new coach and so we didn't really know what to expect.

With all credit to Sharpy, he just picked up from where Tony had left off. It's very difficult to compare the two of them, and it would be wrong to do so in any case.

Sharpy had a lot of his own ideas, and he was young for a coach so he was well in touch with the lads. But he took a good look at the work that had already been done, and he didn't change too much. It was more the case that he built on the things that Tony had done before him, and I think that gave the team more confidence. So a bounce seemed less likely as the season approached.

And for me it was good to work with another coach. It was obvious that coming from Saints he knew what he was talking about. And he coached me personally in a very similar way to Tony. He told me to get on and play my own game and gave me a free role. I slotted in at stand off and hooker from time to time, but I had the licence to run and carry the ball.

I've developed the way I play over time. God knows I've had some things to work on. And I'd like to think I've come a long way since I was running around in my village back home. But you've probably noticed that at the time of writing I've picked up two suspensions already this season. At the time of reading it might be four! But there is one thing that has stayed constant throughout my career and that is the sheer passion I have for the game. I'll put my body on the line time and time again, and it's starting to hurt more now. But I've never been afraid of a fight.

Guys I've played with and against know that I play with pride every time I pull on the shirt. I know I'm aggressive, I'll always be shouting, 'smash him' or 'hit him' when I'm in the defensive line. But back home when warriors take their bow and arrow into battle they don't go just to have a dance. They go to kill people. And if they don't, they'll end up dead themselves. I'm not saying the footy field is a battlefield, I know guys who would, but the way anyone plays on the pitch says a lot about where they have come from, and what is in their mind every hour of the day.

If I play badly that really hurts me. It makes me miserable around the house because my pride has been damaged. But when I play well, and I can see that the supporters are cheering for me, there is no greater high in sport.

And every time I take the field I'm pumped up. Sure I'm shouting, but the opposition is shouting too. I hear them call my name and I know I'm marked, so I know I have to find another way to get away. But I always know I'm in for a battle.

There is no place on the footy pitch for anyone who doesn't have pride.

♦

Towards the end of the previous season, Jo and I had found a house to buy near Huddersfield, and so we had already moved in. We had been thinking about selling our house in Hull for a while, and I had been getting a bit tired of all the journeys up and down the motorway every day. But when I signed the extension to my contract, the club wanted me to move down as well. They said they wanted me to get involved in more sponsorship events and promotions. But I think the truth is that Steve had told them that I was a shit driver, and sooner or later, driving up and down the motorway I was going to kill myself!

So, all things considered, we decided to make the move. And I've always found house hunting very easy over here. People in the UK seem to go on about the area and stuff like that, saying this place is a bad place to live or this one is good. Kirsty and Phil from that 'Location, Location' show have even made a nice living out of it on the telly. And they told everyone that the worst place to live in the country is Hull. But like anyone who has actually lived in Hull, I know what a great place it is. Sure there are bad people everywhere you go, but there are a lot more who are good. Even in the worst places, there are a lot of really good people.

And you have to remember that I come from a place where, when you take a dump, you have to check the toilet for pigs or small children first. So I sometimes think that people over here can get a bit obsessed about the whole thing. You might want to live in some little corner somewhere, where the Mums drive four by fours, all the kids are called Tarquin and everyone talks about money. But I sometimes think that wherever you can find a kebab shop, there are likely to be less people nearby that have got wedged up their own arses. On the other hand there's probably a better chance of getting mugged.

So I think the main thing to remember is that you'll find good and bad wherever you go. It doesn't matter where you are in the whole world. You just have to feel right about the place. When we went to look in Milnsbridge, some of the guys were saying that it's just full of old factories and mills, but I loved it as soon as I saw it. It was so peaceful. And the house we found was just a five minute walk away from a river, so it would be great for me to go fishing. So we moved in and we settled really quickly. In all honesty we didn't have that much time to look for a house. We didn't have weeks or months. We had decided to do it, and then had just a couple of weeks before I went back to PNG for the close season. So I think we landed lucky.

The club was happy that I'd moved, but not half as happy as Steve. I think he'd told Jon and Ken that I shouldn't be driving up and down the motorway as much, because he was fed up of being in the car with me. Steve still lived in Beverley, so before I moved to Milnsbridge, we used to meet at North Cave and then take it in turns to drive down. But Steve was getting a bit sick of it all.

One of the problems was that I have a bit of a tricky habit, or a condition, call it what you like. But everyone that I've played with knows that I have it. There's no delicate way to put it really. I fart a lot. It's the most natural thing in the world for me but some guys think it's funny, and other people think it's out of order, especially in church. It's often said that I do more pumping than North Sea Oil. But I've never been able to understand why I fart more than everyone else. I couldn't understand how guys could play a game of footy so full of air.

But I don't think Steve thought it was all that funny. When it was his turn to drive he used to say, 'whatever you do, don't do it in the car. You've got to respect my family, this is a family car.' So of course I did what I could to help. But on one occasion I went a little bit too far.

Every time we had a game on the Sunday, we always had a nice easy session on the Monday. We'd play a bit of touch rugby and have a warm down and then it was an early finish. This particular day Steve had given me a lift down, but he was doing some extra work at the club so I had an hour or so to kill before we headed back to Hull. And so I went for a little walk with a couple of the boys.

We were going down towards the canal and we went past a hedgerow. Then I noticed that it was packed full of ripe blackberries. I couldn't just walk past them, so I started picking and eating them. I absolutely stuffed myself. And when we came back past the same hedgerow I did it again. I ate as many as I possibly could and the boys were saying, 'hey Stan, stop eating those you'll make yourself sick.'

When Steve eventually picked me up I have to say I was starting to feel just a little bit poorly. And as we sped up the motorway I was feeling steadily worse. I was mindful of the fact that Steve didn't like me to fart in his car, but I was starting to feel really bloated. I thought that I'd have to either sneak a little pump out, or I might be sick. And as always, Steve's car was absolutely gleaming, inside and out.

As we flew past the Castleford exit, I think Steve noticed that I was looking a bit peaky, and I hadn't been talking that much:

"Are you okay Stan?

"No man, I'm not feeling too good at all, I think I'm going to..."

"Oh come on Stanley, don't fart for Christ's sake" Steve was looking genuinely desperate, and I knew how much he hated me spoiling the fresh air in his car, so I promised to do the best I could:

"I feel terrible man, I don't know if I can stop it but I'll give it my best shot."

This was a lot to ask, but we were only twenty minutes or so from my drop off, so I was confident that I could make it. I thought that maybe if I read the paper for a while the time would pass more quickly, but I was feeling even sicker. All I could think about was Steve's clean car, and I knew that he was taking his family out that afternoon. Then, when I seemed to be feeling a bit better, in an entirely involuntary movement, my arse exploded!

It was a funny old feeling. On the one hand I immediately felt less bloated, but then the horrific realisation of the full extent of my guff came over me:

"Er, Steve, I've just shit in my pants."

My whole life flashed before my eyes. At first Steve looked like he was going to pass out. Then he looked like he didn't know whether to laugh or cry. Then he looked like he definitely wasn't going to laugh. And sounding eerily like Clint Eastwood in the Dirty Harry films he hissed:

"Don't get any shit on the car."

The only thing I could think of was to use my newspaper. It seemed a terrible shame to use a copy of the Sun to protect Steve's seats but it was the only thing I could find at this moment of desperation. I used my left hand to lift myself up and slid the paper under my offending arse. A full page picture of the American Ryder Cup team disappeared beneath my soggy trousers.

I don't think Steve said much for the remainder of our trip, but I couldn't hear anything anyway because we had all the windows open. And I have to say that he could have really fallen out with me, but he's a great friend. And I even saw a little smile as I got out of his car at North Cave, with my soiled copy of the Sun, everyone apart from Davis Love the Third now completely obscured.

What a mate I am. Steve had asked me to respect his car and not fart, so what did I do? I crapped in it!

◆

But Steve and I continued to share a car, in spite of my trouser trouble. And believe it or not we still had a hairier moment to come.

In 2003 when we were knocked out of the cup we had a training weekend. This is what we always did if we had a free weekend, we'd go and do something different as a team, somewhere away from the club. This time we were going to Bridlington. I'm pretty sure that Steve must have arranged it, because he lived the closest to the coast. All the boys who lived in Huddersfield and Wakefield had to make the long drive up, but it was a nice change for us to have a short trip.

So I picked Steve up at his house and we headed for the coast. I was quite looking forward to wandering along the beach with some fish and chips, and I'd even packed my beach shorts; but none of it. Jon had a rigorous training schedule planned, and we spent the whole day running along the beach and swimming in the sea. Now I hate swimming at the best of times, but in the sea? We were in the sea for over an hour, and I think we must have run seven or eight miles along the sand. By three o'clock we were all completely knackered. The sea air and the heavy training had left me without any energy and I just wanted to get home to put my feet up. We hadn't even stopped for an ice cream.

Steve must have been bushed as well because he was nodding off in the car all the way home and when we were getting close to Beverley, about fifteen minutes away from his house he said:

"Goodnight Stan."

And I could see him out of the corner of my eye put his head on the door and he was asleep. We were on a winding country road, but I was finding it hard to keep my eyes open. Less than two minutes later I was asleep too.

It was the first and last time I've ever done that when I've been driving, and we so nearly ended up dead. The next thing I knew, I was woken by a terrible noise, a deafening horn and screeching. As I looked up, the first thing I saw was a white transit van right in front of me. The van swerved to the right and

I just managed to haul the car the other way. We hit a kerb, bounced onto a grass bank and came to a stop

Thank God there were no cars behind us and only one van in front. We had just clipped the van on the rear as we both swerved; it was a miracle that we hadn't hit the van full on.

Steve woke with a jolt and was looking around, trying to work out what had happened. When I told him, he was really mad with me, so I said:

"You said 'night night' so I went to sleep!"

"Fucking Hell Stan! You could have killed us both. I could have been dead!"

We both sat there in a state of shock, and then the van drew up just across the road from us. There were two guys in the van. So I was going to have to go and say sorry. We both climbed out of the car and as we were walking across the road, this big guy was coming to meet us. I was going to ask if they were okay but before I could he looked at Steve and said:

"Hi Steve, hi Stan. Hey you wouldn't mind signing this shirt for my little boy would you?"

And with that he handed Steve a black and white shirt and gave us a broad smile.

Steve looked at me and I looked at him and we pissed ourselves. We had nearly died here, and the guy we were going to take with us wanted us to sign a Hull F.C shirt!

To this day Steve always says, 'do you remember that, you nearly killed me?' and I say, 'Mate, every morning when you wake up and you look out of your window at the sky and the sun, and you breathe that first breath of air, thank Mr Gene, because if I hadn't pulled the steering back, you'd be a dead man!' And I think he knows that, because when he became Bradford coach, he still took me there.

But after all his experiences, Steve had no doubt in his mind that I should spend as little time in a car as possible. He should have seen me eight years earlier!

◆

I think Steve and the club were right as it turned out. We settled really well in Milnsbridge, and I started to feel the benefit of not spending half my day on the motorway. I was training well, and getting more time to see Jo and Elliott. And Huddersfield was a good place to be.

The Giants impressed a lot of people that year, by the way we played progressive footy, and showed a lot of fight. Any worries that the supporters had, that we might be on the slide again, were misplaced. We knew what our strengths and limitations were, and as I said, Sharpy carried on the great work that Tony had done before him.

It was always going to be one of the big four to win the league that year; we weren't kidding ourselves about that. But we came close to the top teams throughout the season. And we were particularly good at beating Saints at home. It was always a fixture I looked forward to, and it almost seemed that Sharpy had some kind of hold over his former club. It obviously helped that he knew so much about their players and the way they played.

Saints ended up winning the Challenge Cup that year, but they never fancied coming to the McAlpine Stadium. And we finished just outside the play offs again.

And there was good reason for optimism for the following season, because the squad was getting stronger, and was still quite young. There was obviously a risk that we were going to lose Macca; he was getting slower and slower on the field, and I think after spending two years in the car with me, his nerves were shot!

But while everything was going well at the club, and we had settled happily in the area, I have to say that I was getting a bit distracted towards the end of the season. Christina had rung me from home to tell me that Kaula wasn't well at all, and Maul was very worried for him. That gave me a lot of worry as well; Kaula was eighty and not as strong as he was. So during all the time that things were going so well for me in the UK, a large part of my mind and my heart was on the other side of the world.

At the club we had played so well, and we just missed out on the top six. But I have to be honest when I say that it was a blessing for me. Just before the end of the season I had found out that Kaula had suffered a stroke. And so I wanted to go home straight away. If we had made the play offs I would have been panicking about my dad, and I don't know whether my heart would have been in the game. And I never have, and never will step out onto a pitch with anything less than a strong head on my shoulders and a burning need to win.

As soon as the season was over I flew out at the end of September. Jo understood completely. She knows that there was a big part of Kaula running right through me, and that inside I was frightened. She also knows more than most people what it means to have a family that you can always rely on.

♦

The flight over to PNG seemed longer than ever. Sure, I was looking forward to seeing everyone, but I was anxious to find out how Kaula was. When I arrived at the village, I went to see Christina and Maul, and then I went straight to the hospital.

While I was on the way to the hospital all sorts of things were going through my mind. I hadn't even reached the ward where he was and I was already starting to beat myself up. I didn't know how bad Kaula really was, but Christina had told me he wasn't too good. And then I started to think the worst, and to wish that I had done more things with him when I had grown up. When I was a kid, Kaula was always there for me, taking me out to play footy, going hunting, or just looking for worms. He taught me everything he knew about the land and our country, and never tired of my questions. He seemed to have so much time for me, but I didn't realise that he was working ten hours a day as well.

And I got to thinking that I wished I had spent more time with him over the past few years. I wished that we'd gone out for a beer more, or gone fishing. Or I could have put him in a car and driven him to see the next city, anything to spend time together. It just seemed that I didn't have as much time as I wanted. I was away playing rugby nine months of the year, and back home for eight weeks or so.

But if you sit down and think how much time your dad gave you when you were a kid, it makes you realise just how much you owe him. And I say to anyone who still has their dad, make sure you do what you can, to spend some time with him. At least, take a day off work and go for a good long beer together.

Kaula was always proud of me but he didn't boast. He didn't say, 'I'm Stan's dad' or this and that. If I was walking down the street with my mates and he walked past us, he'd just say 'hi'. He was very modest and he never wanted to be in the way. I wish now that I'd said, 'come here Dad, you're with me, let's go for a beer.'

When I got to the corridor that led to Dad's ward it was a strange feeling. My legs were getting heavier and I could feel my heart pumping. No one wants to see their dad in hospital. And I just wanted to see that he was okay.

And then I saw him in the corner of the room. He looked eighty years old for the first time in his life. But when he saw me, he moved his head up and I went straight over to give him the hug that I had wanted to give for the past week. And then I sat down.

I could see what the stroke had done to Kaula. The right side of his face was dead, and he was finding it hard to move. He could speak a bit, but sometimes his tongue didn't really work and so he got angry. And so he talked by nodding or shaking his head when I asked him questions.

I spent a lot of time with Kaula over the next few weeks, and we talked about just about everything. But I could see that a lot of the time he was tired, and so it worried me that he wasn't getting any better. And I didn't want to leave him when the time came. So I told him that I would miss the pre-season training, and stay on to be with him.

But Kaula wouldn't have any of that. He was quite firm and tried to tell me that I had to go to training. He said to me, 'I'm happy. And if I hear that you're playing rugby I'll always be

World Club Champion with Bradford Bulls 2006

The Goroka Team 1994. I'm the one who's not paying attention

PNG Kumulus Team with Adrian Lam front row 3rd from left

Back home and dressed for dinner!

I'm always proud to wear PNG Kumulus colours

happy. So go back to England'. He was very proud of me, and that just made me want to do whatever he asked.

I knew that he was right in a lot of ways. There wasn't much I could do to help over there, but I wanted to spend as much time with Kaula as I could. He talked to me about where he wanted to be buried. That's kind of a hard thing for a son to hear from his dad, but old people often seem quite matter of fact about stuff like that. He wanted to go back to the village where he was born. If he died in Goroka, he didn't want to be buried there, he wanted to go back home. He had spent a lot of his time in the village, and that's where he wanted to rest.

I said to him, 'when the time comes, I'll fly you back to the village in a chopper,' and when I said that I could see that he was trying to smile. And I wasn't joking. He was loved by everyone in the village, and his name was known throughout PNG and around the world. It was definitely the right thing to do.

So I flew back to England for Christmas and in a lot of ways I felt happier that I'd had so much time with Kaula. There was a big part of me that wondered if I would ever see him again. But it was great to spend Christmas with my own family back in Milnsbridge and I started to prepare as usual for the new season.

The pre-season training camp was in Portugal, and I was hoping the weather would be warmer than in Yorkshire. I still can't get used to the cold over here, and that year it was just the same as usual – bloody freezing. I'd been out for a few runs around Slaithwaite, but I always had about four layers of clothes to keep me warm.

And my thoughts were turning to the new season, but just as I was preparing for the pre-season training, another bolt hit me. Kaula had a second stroke. I got to know pretty quickly, because the doctor who had been called out to attend to him recognised the name, and he rang Uncle Dixon straight away. My uncle then rang me and I was in turmoil again.

But thank God the doctor had contacted us so quickly. I telephoned the hospital and got put through to Dad's ward and I managed to speak to him. I said, 'hey don't panic Dad, we planned your funeral when I was over there.' It was kind of an odd thing to say but I knew he was worried about that and I just wanted to tell him things that would make him happy. I still hoped that his funeral would be a long time away.

I found it hard to understand Dad on the phone and when he rang off I telephoned Christina. She told me that he was going to go soon. So I told Jo and we just had to prepare ourselves for what was coming next.

But as the days went on Dad's condition seemed to have stabilized; I didn't hear anything other, and so the week before the team was due to fly to Portugal I went down to London to get my Visa. This is something I always have to do before we play in France, or anywhere abroad, because my PNG passport doesn't work there!

We were back in training the week before we were scheduled to fly to Portugal. But I remember one morning I got a call from my uncle. I could tell from the tone of his voice that I was going to get the news that I'd sort of being expecting, but had put to the back of my mind.

Kaula had gone.

Sharpy pulled me into his office, because he'd got an email at the club in the morning telling him my news. He didn't know that I already knew that Kaula was dead and I could see that he was struggling to know what to say to me. But I just said to him, 'look mate I've got to go' and he was great about it all. So I never got to Portugal that year. It's weird because we went for pre-season training there with Rovers this year and I saw a signed Giants shirt. It just took me back to that time, and of course my signature wasn't on the shirt.

I didn't go straight home. I just hung around the club a little, because I didn't really know what to do with myself. I don't think it had really hit me properly, because when I did arrive home it all came out of me. Jo could see that I was devastated and she didn't know how to fix things. But nobody could have fixed it. My dad was dead.

I was really angry with myself because normally I don't show too many emotions, and I try to be as strong as I can. But Jo knew how close I was to Kaula and Maul and she understood. I felt like something had burnt right through the middle of me and left a big hole. But I had to get myself together as quickly as I could. So I took it all in and decided what to do next.

♦

I had to organise the funeral. And I didn't know anything about funerals, but I was desperate to make sure that I did everything right for Kaula. The most important thing for me was to remember my promise to him to fly his body back to the village in a helicopter. So the next day, I spoke to someone at Goroka Airport and it was all arranged. I was so keen for this to happen, because sometimes it can be very rainy up in the mountains and difficult to drive. And I didn't want his coffin to be bouncing around; I just wanted him to have the send off that he deserved.

Two days later I was on a flight to PNG. I took Elliott with me. He wanted to come and Jo said it was alright, so off we went. It was a long flight as always, especially long for a little boy, but he was really good company for me. We flew from Manchester to Singapore, and then on to Port Moresby, before finishing our journey at Goroka. The chopper was waiting for us at Goroka Airport, but our flight from the capital was delayed.

I rang my uncle to tell them not to wait for us, to set off and we'd see them later, but inside I was gutted. The pilot waited for as long as he could, but then eventually had to make the call to set off. He knew that in the afternoons it's often very cloudy up there, and he wouldn't be able to gain enough height to get clear.

We were about an hour late, and as we landed we could see the chopper taking off. So we dumped our bags in the boot of a hire car and drove up towards the mountains.

I thank God that Kaula had just the sort of funeral that I had wanted for him. In life, he was a humble man, but hugely respected by everyone he met. And as the story passed around, people in the surrounding villages got to know that he was coming home in a chopper. This was the first time anyone had ever been flown back in a helicopter, and the first time that most of the villagers had seen one.

So as the noise of the whirring blades filled the air above the opening where the chopper could land, rows and rows of tribes from the nearby villages appeared from behind the trees. Many chiefs had come to pay their respects, and three or four churches were there too, taking it in turns to play songs. I know that it meant the world to Maul to see Kaula come home to his rest this way.

And Kaula's funeral was very different in another way. Usually in PNG funerals last one or two weeks. There is often a week of mourning and crying, and then after the body is buried, another week of tributes. I didn't really want to change the way we had funerals, but life is changing all the time all around the world, and very much in PNG, so I decided the whole occasion should be short and sharp. I didn't really have a choice, because the club wanted me back in England as soon as possible. And also, life was getting tougher back home in PNG, and to provide food for so many people for two weeks would cost a lot of money.

It's hard to organise something like this because it's not like in England where there's always a buffet, whether it's a funeral, a wedding or a christening. People bring food and some bring money, and the ones who bring money take away some food, a bunch of bananas or even a pig. So if three or four hundred people turn up and there's not enough food to go round you will get a bad name.

The next day, Maul's closest friends came back and we gave them all food to take away, as a thank you for all their help. And then we put him in the ground.

The following day I took Elliott back to England. On the way we had two nights in Goroka and a night at Port Moresby. I thought that he had seen enough of the funeral; it's quite a hard thing for a nine year old to take in. But again, I was proud of the way he was with my family and the people in the village. He fits in there so easily.

While we were in Goroka, I heard that some of Dad's oldest friends were unhappy because they had missed the funeral. Some of the boys he had grown up with had moved to Lae, and couldn't get to the village in time. I felt bad about that, but I didn't think that there was anything else I could have done at the time. But the next year I called his old mates and gathered them together in the village and we had a Mumu. It was a way of his friends saying goodbye and paying their own respects. They put some stones in a hole in the ground and placed some sticks across the top to make a fire. And on top of this they cooked a stew with pork and cabbage and spices. Then we had a few beers and all the old boys were happy.

I was relieved that Kaula had the send off that he deserved, and I had managed to say goodbye to the greatest man I knew, in just the way I wanted.

♦

I was pleased to see Jo again when we got home, and now I was just looking forward to getting back to a normal life. Losing your dad is one of the hardest things you ever have to go through, but it is all part of what makes you the person you are. I think it's a big step for guys because you realise that now you're the head of the family, and you're the dad. I know that girls sometimes say that guys never actually grow up, but if that's the case, you get pretty damn close at times like this.

I had to start training really hard because I'd missed the whole of the pre-season. The boys told me that it had gone well in Portugal, and I could sense that the club was quietly growing in ambition. Huddersfield has sometimes struggled to get big crowds, I guess because they are so close to Leeds, Bradford and Wakefield. And there are loads of lower level clubs nearby as well. And someone told me that the football club was a great team once and they have quite a big following. West Yorkshire is a hotbed of sport. But Rugby League is a lot stronger than soccer at the minute, there isn't one Yorkshire team in the Premier League. And the great thing for us in the north east is that the team that are closest to reaching the top level is Hull City. Success for the big sports clubs makes such a difference to how people feel about their town. And to have three clubs in the city that are in their top divisions would be brilliant.

The Giants had steadily progressed over the past three years and under Ken Davy's guidance, this had carried on in a quiet, sensible way. Sharpy hadn't made sweeping changes when he arrived, and again at the beginning of the 2005 season he just added one or two players. But they were real quality, especially Brad Drew who came over from Australia.

And I soon came to be enjoying my rugby again. I was playing in a team that was competitive in the Super League, and could hold their own against most of the league. I was probably playing the best footy of my career at this point. I wasn't scoring as often as I did when I was younger, but through the guidance of Tony and now Sharpy I was much more of a team player. I still had a free role in a lot of the games, and covered a lot of ground, and while I only scored seven tries that year I found loads of opportunities for my mates.

Another thing I started to find as I got older was that I was getting injured more. Thank God I've always recovered from injuries quickly, but this year in particular I got to know the medical staff very well. The physio was a guy called Martin. He was a great kid and he knew how my body worked inside and out. Even when Tony was at the club I was regularly having treatment. Tony joked that whenever the boys came into the gym to do some weight training, I was always having a snooze on the physio's table. And he was probably right. Martin and Dr Ahmed were on my British Telecom 'friends and family' list, along with Jo, the Lucky Star and Dominos Pizza.

Martin's a really good guy and he knows how to make the best of his life. At the end of the season he took a year out to travel round the world. He went to live in Bali and spent a lot of time in Australia. And the great thing is, when he got back to England, Macca rang him up and he went to be the physio at Bradford.

And we had this brilliant masseur called Steve. The boys all had twenty minute sessions with Steve, but of course I had thirty.

To be fair all the coaches I have worked with will probably say I'm not the greatest believer in training, and they're absolutely right. I'd much rather be playing matches, but then again who wouldn't?

We played consistently good footy all the way through the season, and we finished up in a similar position to the year before. We were never in danger of going down and sat in mid table at the end. I thought that I was part of an emerging club, and about two thirds of the way through the year I started to think about where I wanted to be.

At the end of this season I had one more year to run on my contract, and after I'd discussed it with Jo, I went to see Sharpy to ask for an extension to take me to the end of 2007. It was all those endless journeys with Macca up and down the M62, when he was telling me about security and asking me not to fart. I think that had finally rubbed off on me. And I was confident that I would get another year. I had been there at the start of the revolution under Tony and had four good seasons there, improving with the team.

So I didn't take it too well when I was told that there was nothing doing. I guess he had his reasons. And I could see, talking to the other boys that he was clearing out some of the older guys, to make room for some youngsters. But Macca had already gone so the average age of the team had dropped by about five, and I think Sharpy must have thought I was older than I am! You shouldn't believe everything that you read in the papers.

I thought that the squad had a very good balance, but clearly Sharpy wanted to take the club in a new direction. And I wasn't going to be part of his long term plans. I told him that he should know that you never win anything with kids.

But in all seriousness when I was told I wouldn't get another year I felt pretty insulted. At the point that I had signed the previous contract, I was upset that Tony was leaving the club and I did have other offers to consider. So I helped out at a time when I was needed and, in any case, I did think I was worth an extension. But rugby clubs are like any other business, and the manager can bring in whoever he wants.

I had another year on my contract to run, but I honestly felt like I'd been kicked in the face. I don't know if the fact that I'd lost my dad earlier in the year had brought me down, but I was completely pissed off. All sorts of things were going on in my head, and I just kept telling myself to stay focused to the end of the season and then think again.

But it seems that whoever is looking out for me up there was on top of the situation. And, like so often before, something happened to take me in another direction. And like so often before, it was completely out of my control. After training one day Sharpy called me over for a quick word:

"Stan, how do you fancy a move to Bradford?"

This came like a bolt out of the blue. I couldn't understand why Bradford would come in for me at this time. I knew that Macca was there as Brian Noble's assistant, so they knew about me, but this was the first I'd heard of any serious interest.

But it was absolutely true. It turns out that Sharpy was after Robbie Paul and he had a year left on his contract at Bradford. As I was in the same boat the two clubs agreed to do a straight swap. And for me it was a no-brainer. The move was very smooth as everybody was happy with the deal from the very beginning.

It had happened again. Every time in my career that the time was right for a move, somebody did all the work for me! And in many ways this was the biggest move of all. It was a fantastic offer. I got a two year contract and an option for a third, and Bradford were an awesome side. They won the league in 2005 and as soon as the deal was signed I started dreaming. It really might be that the first game I played for the Bulls would be in the World Club Championship!

It seemed like as I was getting older I was moving on to better things. And as I prepared to make my end of season trip back home, I couldn't help but think what an incredible year it had been. The beginning of the year was the worst time of my life. But I was making my way to the airport as a Bradford player.

This was the best team in the country, and maybe even the world.

10

Drowning not Waving

2006
Bradford

Every time I go home I still get excited, and in some ways it's got better as I get older. All the fuss of the first couple of visits was nice, but it would drive you mental if that happened every time. And so now when I go home I have more time to spend with my family.

But this time was different in three ways. Firstly, I had so much exciting stuff to tell the folks back home. I'd just signed for Bradford, the best team in the UK, and there was a great chance that I would be playing in the World Club Championship in the New Year. Even when I was on the flight to PNG, I was already looking forward to going back to training. And that was something of a miracle in itself! But there the second difference hit me really hard. The one guy that I wanted to tell the most wasn't going to be there. Sure, all the rest of the boys would be on top of the world, but sometimes when I sat down, I just couldn't believe that Kaula had passed away. It still hits me now from time to time.

But that's the way of the world. 'The circle of life' or whatever it's called. I don't have any grandparents in the village now. It does make my suitcase lighter, because I always used to take rice home for them all. But I guess I'd rather have a heavy suitcase.

And there was another guy I was going to see this time around. A guy that I never knew about, that I never cared about, but one that did have quite an important part in my story. Mum had telephoned me before I took off to say that he was already there, so that I wasn't going to be too shocked when I arrived. But I didn't really know what to think. After all, I'd never met the guy before so why should I care? I suppose it was the fact that he happened to be there when my mum got pregnant over thirty years ago. But by the time I splashed onto the scene nine months later he was gone.

And this time around, the bastard did it again! Robert (it seemed funny to find out the name of my biological dad) was already in the village with Mum when I set off from the UK. He'd actually been there before, and I didn't have a clue how many times. You'll have the idea by now that for some reason back home, I'm always the last to find out, particularly things of massive importance to me. Don't ask me why.

He'd actually been there at Kaula's funeral! To be fair, there were so many people there, and I didn't know them all, so he just kind of blended in.

But when I arrived at Mum's there was no sign of the Scarlett bloody Pimpernel. Mum told me that when he heard that I was due to land he did a runner. The poor sod thought that I was going to beat him up. And in all honesty he was possibly right. He thought that it would be a good idea for Mum to tell me that he'd been around again, and test the water with me.

As it turned out, that was the right thing to do, because when I saw that Christina was okay with it, and actually he'd been around a little more than I knew, I was happy to meet him. In fact I wanted to.

How often Robert had been around I'll never know, but it was a least twice. Family lines are not as clearly drawn back home as they are in the UK, with the possible exception of Lincolnshire. So when Ben was born, I thought of course that he was my cousin, but then when he was five years older he suddenly became my brother. And guess who his dad was. Bulls eye – so to speak.

When Mum told me this I started to catch on. I had never asked questions of her, and thought that if she wanted to tell me something she would. To be honest, I had even found out that she was my Mum by accident, thanks to Judy's big mouth. But I was getting the hang of it now. Five years after Ben was born Mum was pregnant again, and when Martin arrived I thought I had a new half brother. But now the realisation fell over me. Dead Eye Dick had hit the target again and all three of us had the same dad. And hats off to the guy, because all this time he was working in Lae, some five hours drive away.

♦

After I'd had the chance to think about it all, I didn't have any bad feelings towards Robert. He hadn't done anything wrong to me. In fact, I had quite a lot to thank him for! It was a funny thing really; because we'd never talked about him, and I had no idea who he was, so I never felt like I was missing anything. And of course, I had the greatest dad anyone could ever want in Kaula, and nothing could ever change that. Kaula was my dad and Robert was the guy who'd made it all possible, so why have any bad feelings?

But when I first saw Robert I could see that he wasn't convinced that I'd be cool. I could see in his eyes that he was thinking, 'is he gonna beat the shit out of me?'

I guessed he was about fifty. He certainly looked older than Christina, and I tried to work out how old he was when I was born, but I couldn't. He didn't look like he had spent his life working on the land. Which, in fact, he hadn't. He had worked for Toyota, mainly in Lae for all the time that he had been away. I think he had a pretty good job selling cars. And he could certainly speak very good English, although you wouldn't know that at the very first moment that I met him.

It was when I was sat in Mum's house one afternoon. It was a day or two after she'd spoken to me about Robert. And then I heard two people coming up to the door. And there he was. I could hardly believe my eyes. He was a little bald guy and he was absolutely shitting himself. He didn't even look at me; his eyes were staring downward at the floor. I don't think it was just the fact that he was my dad that was churning him up. He also knew that back home I was a pretty powerful guy. And it turned out that he had been around, seeing Christina more regularly than I thought. So he had heard one or two stories of fights I'd been in and I think he was expecting the same kind of reception.

You have to remember too that he was chased away from the village all those years ago, so he had no idea what the limit of the angry feeling was. And it was no coincidence that he made his first public appearance after Kaula had died. The truth of it was that when he did come back, about seventy percent of the village was not pleased. So I guess that took some balls in the first place. And as I said before, he hadn't committed a terrible crime. He'd just done what millions of guys in PNG, and around the world, had done before him. Not nice, but hardly a capital offence.

There was a part of me that was angry inside, but the bigger part just wanted to see what he was like. I guess if I'd had a couple of beers I would have pinned him to the wall and scared the shit out of him, but in a lot of ways I'm older and wiser now.

So I held out my hand to him and he looked into my eyes for the very first time. It was the weirdest thing.

I always laugh at those daytime programmes in the UK where they have a feature called 'I haven't seen my dad for ten years' or something, and they have a studio audience cheering. Then this smooth guy comes on and sticks his microphone in the face of a skinhead with a union jack tattooed on his head, and everyone boos. It's like a pantomime but without the ice creams. The best ones are 'I didn't realise my wife of twenty years was a man' – when the 'wife' has bigger hands than Joe Vagana!

Anyway, back in Segu there was no studio audience and Jeremy Kyle was nowhere to be seen, but I did my best without him. I looked him right in the eyes and said:

"Where the fuck have you been for the last thirty years? You know now you're going to have to spend your time cooking and washing and cleaning. Just like Christina's been doing all the time you've been away."

He looked at me now, and started speaking in English:
"I have. That's exactly what I've been doing for the last three months."

So that was it. I'd finally met my dad and in all honesty, it just wasn't a big deal. That's why I'll never get on daytime telly I suppose. I just gave him a hug and said 'well it's nice to see you' and from then we just got along.

And the funny thing is that he was telling the truth. In the months that he'd been living with Christina he had been doing all the housework, and it turned out that he was a great cook as well. No disrespect to Christina, but I kind of wished he'd been around a bit longer, everyone knows how important my stomach is to me!

And over the past couple of years I've got on okay with Robert on the few times I've met him. He always speaks proper English to me and I'm happy to share a few beers with him. He said to me that he was going to come and meet me a long time ago, but Kaula was still there and he remembered being chased out of the village. That doesn't matter to me at all. I'd got along just fine for over thirty years, but it was nice to meet him anyway.

You can't change what's in the past; you just have to make the best of every day as it comes. It's a simple philosophy but I can't see what's wrong with it.

But as the days went on, I got on better and better with Robert. I used to laugh at him doing all the cleaning and cooking, and bickering with Christina. She was always pushing him around. It looked like they had been married all their lives!

Sometimes in the afternoons we'd have a few beers together. I was on holiday and he could see I was getting bored so we'd send the boys out to get some beers and a bag of ice. Then we'd put the ice in a pot and throw the beers in and while away the afternoon listening to the sounds of the bush and just talking. That's often the way that people open out and I got to know him pretty well.

He told me how he used to meet Christina, but because he couldn't come to the village, or even Goroka, they had to speak on the phone and arrange to meet somewhere else. When I was growing up I couldn't understand why Christina didn't have a man in the village. But Robert was her first boyfriend and she never had anyone else. She always says, 'I have three boys; what do I need a man for?'

I'd love to know how they met up without any of us knowing.

And at the end of the long afternoons, when Christina arrived home from work I'd shout at Robert, 'hey Mum's home, you should have some food on the table!'

We got on well and I sort of wish I'd known him when I was younger.

Later that year Mum told me that he'd got fed up and gone back to work in Lae. He'd split up with his wife and now he had a new girl in Lae. I know Mum still speaks to him on the phone and I think she feels sorry for him.

♦

Pre-season training started straight after Christmas, and I had never had a start like this before. The training was geared up to our first match, which happened to be the World Club Championship against West Tigers at Huddersfield. I couldn't believe that at this stage in my career I was heading for such a big season at a massive club.

And even better for me, I had the chance to play alongside my old mate Marcus Bai. This was such a fantastic thing because I never thought I'd get the chance to play alongside Marcus. We played for PNG Kumuls together but never for the same club before. It's really weird because Marcus came over to Hull at the same time as I came with John Okul to join Hull KR. But he went to play for Hull F.C. He didn't quite make it there and soon I heard he was playing for Hull Dockers under-21 side.

After that he went back home, but within a year he had trials with Gold Coast, and from there he went on to Melbourne Storm where he really made a name for himself. He's still a legend in Melbourne now. When he came over to play for Leeds we got in touch again. I was in Huddersfield so he used to bring his family over to see us. It was always great fun when we got together; we could talk our own language and have a good laugh. And I couldn't wait to line up alongside him for Bradford.

But I was brought back down to earth pretty quickly when my knee was causing me lots of problems. This is something I've found happening more often through my career. Rugby League is a very tough game, and injuries are easy to pick up. I'd had my fair share but I usually managed to recover quicker than expected. But it was getting harder as I got older and this time I knew I was heading for an operation. I always get pissed off when I'm injured, but this was worse than usual.

Just a week before the match I went in for keyhole surgery which cleared up some bits on my cartilage, and I was still hopeful of making the game. So I went to see Brian Noble, our coach, to let him know how I'd gone on. I don't think he quite believed me when I said I wanted to play, but I was certain in my own mind:

"Brian, you've got to play me. I've never played in a game as big as this in my life, and I don't know if it'll ever come round again. I might never get another chance like this"

I was almost pleading with him. But Brian had already had the report from the specialist and he looked doubtful:

"Come on Stan, it's going to be three weeks, two at the very least."

I wasn't having any of it:

"I don't care! I just want to play in this game Brian."

I'd like to think that he knew I had a better chance than anyone of recovering from an injury in time for this game. But it maybe that he thought I might cry and he didn't want to be embarrassed! So eventually he said 'okay' and we'd look at the progress through the week. Brian had almost convinced me that it was a bridge too far, but I always believed I could get there.

It was also a psychological thing for me. I thought that if I could heal up from this quickly, then I would be okay for the season. And I was desperate to play as much as I could. I pictured myself walking out in front of the packed crowds week after week and I just got more determined.

♦

On the day of the game my dreams had come true. I made it. Okay I didn't start the match but I was on the bench and I knew that I'd get on at some stage. That was if I could get all my layers of kit off in time. It was a night game in Huddersfield and there was a big crowd. I've heard guys say that there's always a special atmosphere at night games, with the floodlights and stuff. But to me it's just even colder than normal. In Huddersfield in February you can freeze your bollocks off in the middle of the day, so why make it even colder?

But maybe that helped my knee! I'd spent half the last week with ice on it and so maybe the colder the better. I know it's unlikely but it seemed that way anyway, because when I got on I couldn't feel a thing and I could run and take hits as well as I ever could.

This was a world class team I was playing for and it inspired me to play my best footy. I couldn't have asked for a better start when we won the World Club Championship and I went over for my first try in Bradford colours.

I spoke to Professor Rolf, the specialist, after the match, and he still couldn't believe that I'd made the game. But that set the tone for my season. Every time I ran out for Bradford I felt like I'd reached the top. I was playing for the best team in the world and I was determined to make the most of every opportunity that came my way.

The whole thing was so great and I settled into the team really quickly. In fact, I'd never played with so many South Sea Islanders in my life. As well as Marcus, there were massive guys there like Joe Vagana, and of course Lesley Vainikolo. Lesley's an incredible man. They call him 'Da Volcano' and you can see why when he explodes on the pitch. He's the most powerful player to come from Tonga in my lifetime. But he's a very spiritual guy as well. When I'd lived over here for ten years I'd sometimes forgotten how religious we all are back home. A lot more people go to church and Lesley brought his faith with him. Before our first match at Huddersfield he took his bible book into the changing room, and he sat down and quietly read a chapter or a verse and then he prayed, before he went out and half killed a few blokes! He does this before every game, but I hadn't seen it before in England.

It's fantastic that Lesley has done so well over here. He's made the switch to Union as well as anyone I've seen, and I'm not at all surprised that he's made the England team. I've often heard it said, but it really couldn't have happened to a nicer guy. He still gets up when he can to see us. He was always one for getting the South Sea Island blokes together when we were all around Leeds. He'd be the first to say, 'hey Wontok, all round to mine for a spit roast.' Any Premier League footballers reading this – it's maybe not what you think lads.

All our families would get together and we'd get a pig from the nearest farm. It was as near to a feast from back home as we could get. And we didn't even have to kill the pig!

And Lesley can eat even more than I can. I remember one time we were having a roast. We'd all had a few beers and I said to him, 'hey there's a whole leg left on the pig.' So he just snapped off the leg and ate it! If the world food shortage ever hits the UK, just make sure you don't live near Da Volcano.

It was good to talk in Pidgin from time to time. We weren't being ignorant to the white guys at all. But sometimes it's nice to remember things from back home when you're so many thousands of miles away. It was the first time over here that I'd been called 'Wantok' which in our language means 'friend'.

One of the best guys in Rugby was there at Bradford as well. Some people think of him as a bit of a bastard on the pitch, but off the pitch Terry Newton is one of the nicest blokes you could ever meet. And there was of course my old mate Macca, waiting to greet me. I think he only talked Brian into bringing me in because I had a house in Huddersfield and he wouldn't have to drive me around any more! He was still smarting from our two accidents a couple of years ago. But it was great to be working with Macca again.

Actually I felt welcome the minute I walked into the club. There was no way I could have really made a quiet entrance. I went into the recreation room at Rawdon and the first thing Terry Newton said to me was:

"Hi Stan, how's the fishing going?"

I'd never met the guy before so I thought this was a bit of a strange greeting. And then Joe said:
"Are you still fishing Stan?"

A couple more fishing comments and I was starting to smell a rat. And then I saw the lad who watched me hurl my fishing rod into the East Park Lake ten years earlier. Matty Brooks was standing with some boys at the pool table and pissing himself. The only effect of me protesting, 'hey I'm pretty good at fishing now' was to send the whole room into helpless guffawing!

♦

The way the club was set up really opened my eyes. For the first time in my career, when I arrived at Rawdon for training I just came in my normal clothes, jeans and stuff. All our training kit was at the club, washed and pressed and laid out for us. After training we just chucked in into a basket and the next day it came back clean again. Jo thought it was great as well!

But the best thing of all for me was the club restaurant. I couldn't believe my eyes when I first walked in there. There were all sorts of stuff prepared – chicken, steaks, all kinds of pasta and salads. There were no tree worms and cabbage but everything else was there and I was in food heaven.

It took me back to my early days at Hull KR when I used to get a full mixed grill when all the rest of the boys were eating gammon. I could stack my plate up and then go back for more. It was like a wedding buffet but with the ugliest set of guests I'd ever seen.

I don't think I cooked a meal at home all year and Jo thought I had a tapeworm! And by the end of the year all the boys at the club called me 'Freefood'. It's nice to make your name at such a big club however you do it.

The way I saw it, the training schedule was pretty tough so it was always important to get my energy back with a big meal.

To be fair, the whole set up was very professional. It was by far the classiest organisation I had seen. They looked after everything the players needed and I'm sure getting that kind of treatment pays off on the pitch. But not every club can afford to do that otherwise I think they probably would.

There was a guy there called Stuart Duffy, he was sort of a general manager. Anything you needed that wasn't rugby related he could sort out for you. He was always available and I still ring him now for advice from time to time. That kind of care in all aspects of the club sums up how Bradford Bulls operates.

But there was a difference that I wasn't used to. And that was the supporters' relationship with the club. They were very passionate and created a brilliant atmosphere, but at the end of the game they all left, and we didn't see them again until the next game. I think that's an area where Hull KR knocks the pants off every other club in the Super League. At Craven Park, after the game, there'll be hundreds of fans staying around, having a drink at the club. And we see them through the week; I know a lot of the fans personally. There is a real family feel about Hull KR. I know I'm sentimental about that, but when you're better than everyone else at something, you've got to shout about it.

It was great to be with Macca again. He was doing a fantastic job as Brian's assistant and I was looking forward to having the crack with him again. Steve knew me well and knew that I liked a laugh and I was always kidding around. But he had taken on a different position and he was now coaching and commanding respect from guys he'd played with and played against. I could see that he wanted a word with me before our first training session, but I didn't really expect what was coming:

"Stanley it's good to have you here mate and we're going to have a great season."

And?

"Well the thing is I've got a big responsibility here coaching these guys, and the last thing I need you to do is to be pissing around, and laughing and joking with me all the time."

I was tempted to say, 'can I not even shit in your car?' but I had recognised that Steve was kind of serious. It had always been a driving ambition of his to become a coach. And I knew he had everything he needed to make a success of it. And I suppose, the least I could do, as a mate, and one that owed him a hell of a lot, was to give him my full support. So all plans of setting fire to his newspaper or farting in his team talks were immediately shelved. My maturity has no limits! And there was no risk of me leaving my mobile on in meetings.

Macca's still a great mate but you have to understand the professionalism that's needed from someone in that position. And he expects it from the team as well. In a winning team there are plenty of laughs to be had, but at the right time, and when we cross the white line then things are deadly serious. And Macca's a winner. But when it was just me and him we could still have the crack, and in many ways that's just as important in life.

I reminded Macca as soon as I arrived at Bradford that I didn't really do training. But Macca said, 'no you'll love it here, it's different.' He was of course lying. It was just the same as training everywhere else, but worse. I had a partner in crime because Joe Vagana was just as keen not to train as me. But even with a mate I had no chance of getting out of anything that Macca cooked up.

We seemed to spend most of our time swimming and rowing, and that kills me. And Macca knew very well that I can't swim. When I jump in the pool I just sink, I can't swim at all - I'm a mountain man for God's sake. Actually, that's not quite true; I can swim under water, but I've never managed to convince any coach that's as good as swimming on the surface. Whenever we go in the pool I just splash around and do what I guess you'd call a doggy paddle.

The worst training experience I ever had was up in Hull when I was playing for Hull F.C. Someone came up with the crazy plan that we should do a triathlon. The idea was to swim ten lengths of the pool, then get on our bikes outside to cycle ten miles or so, then do a run. What an absolutely stupid idea.

Anyway, we all lined up in the pool, ready to jump in and do our ten lengths. Shaun knew what a shit swimmer I was, and he was kinder than Macca, so I only had to do two lengths. And I had a big black rubber ring round my waist that they usually used for the 'family fun splash'. My plan was to get the whole pissing nightmare over as quickly as possible. So I doggy paddled as quickly as my arms would propel me. I lost control a few times when the massive rubber ring drifted on the waves that the other guys were making as they splashed passed me. At one point I started floating backwards, but then my ring drifted into the slipstream of the guy next to me and I was away again. I tried to grab onto someone's foot but I just got a kick in the face.

When I eventually staggered out of the pool, spewing water as I dropped my ring, I could see that Steve Prescott, who was in the lead of the others, had just completed his eighth length. So I had to get a move on to keep my lead. I thought that if I could stay ahead during the bike ride, maybe, just maybe I had a chance. I couldn't actually believe that I was even thinking of that, or taking the whole joke seriously.

I ran outside, still drying myself and then the cold hit me. It was bloody freezing. So I wrapped my towel around me, clambered onto my bike and sped off. I'd only gone about a hundred metres when I saw some other guys getting on their bikes. And it was that moment that my chances of glory came to a crashing end. The end of the towel that I'd wrapped around me dropped down and got tangled in the spokes of my back wheel. And so I went arse over tit, as Steve whizzed past me wobbling as he pissed himself.

♦

The season was going okay for us, but every week that I stepped out in Bradford colours I was swelling with pride. I kept on sending newspaper cuttings back home to Mum and Ben, and they loved seeing that we were often getting headlines in the big national newspapers.

The matches I remember the most were the derbies we had with Leeds Rhinos. They were fierce and the crowds were fantastic. They were real top of the table games and the whole team looked forward to them. The first one at Bradford turned out to be a big disappointment for me, and the club as a whole. We were League Champions and World Club Champions; but we'd just been turned over at home by our local rivals.

Derbys are always the best matches to be involved in. Whether it's Leeds – Bradford or Rovers against Hull the atmosphere's always electric. You can see how much it matters to the fans in the week building up and sometimes things get too heated. I'm not saying that it's as dangerous as a derby in PNG, but when Hull came to Craven Park last year it did get a bit out of hand.

And whenever you hear fans slagging off their coach on the radio, it's quite often just after a derby defeat. But the other side of it is that when you win it couldn't be better. The Leeds players and supporters had a party. The sight of the Leeds fans singing and cheering was enough to make our fans choke on their Yorkshire puddings. And we had some soul searching to do.

We weren't the only ones that were thinking hard. About half way through the season we heard that Brian was going to Wigan and taking Stuart Fielden with him. Wigan was struggling and I think they must have worked very hard to tempt Brian away. But away he went. And that left Macca in complete charge.

And just as I expected, Macca took the chance with both hands. He'd never been the head coach at any team before, and now he was coach at the World Club Champions. I think it raised a few eyebrows in the game, but I know that Steve could have got a job at other places. Both Hull KR and Hull were watching him so Bradford were right to give him the chance. It was everything he had worked so hard to get, and he wasn't about to screw it up.

And he did a brilliant job. Apart from carrying on with the swimming sessions he was doing everything right. And we also got our revenge on Leeds. After the disappointment at home, we went back there and beat them in the last minute. All the players and fans went crazy; it was like winning a Grand Final. And it was all the sweeter because we managed to do just what they had done to us at our place. You only remember the last match when it comes to local derbies. Everyone goes to work on the Monday and in all the factories and offices one half of the staff is grinning, while the other half are complaining or getting on with their work!

I was having the time of my life. I loved the whole experience, the footy was great and the fans were being really good to me. Jo was happy too and we were really settled in our home. It seemed that on the family side, after losing Kaula, and finding Robert, that things were finally calming down. Then one day, while I was getting my stuff together for an afternoon fishing trip, Jo looked at me and turned my world upside down – again:

"I'm pregnant Stan"

Well that was going to put an end to my easy afternoons. Elliott was ten now and the days of wiping shitty arses were a distant memory (apart from in Steve's car of course).

We were both delighted by the news and it seemed that things couldn't get any better. Macca's talks to me all those times on the motorway were paying dividends too. I started to think about the future again. I had another year after this to run on my contract, and I was determined to earn an extension.

And Macca had got the team working well, so we made it to the playoffs at the end of the season. It was no surprise for such a strong team, but Macca still had to do it. In some ways it was a no win situation for him in his first year because the expectation levels were so high.

When the play off came at Hull, I was injured and so had to watch from the sidelines. It was a really frustrating day because we had the game in our hands. Macca was furious, because he knew, like all the rest of us that we could, and should, have gone all the way.

That one year at Bradford was, in a lot of ways, the peak of my career. It was the best footy team I'd played for and I thank God I had the chance to do that. It was brilliant to play with so many world class players and so many South Sea Islanders. And the fans were great as well; I didn't get to know many of them, but they sometimes chanted my name, which meant a lot to me.

I sometimes wish that I could have turned back the clock, and that I'd gone to Bradford earlier in my career. I had a good time wherever I went and I can only think of two or three years that I could have 'given away'.   But I wonder what I could have achieved if I'd been at the club for three or four years. Who knows?

And at the end of the day I still had another year to play on my contract. I was very confident that I could play an important part in this team. In my first year I'd made twenty-four appearances and gone over to score ten times. So I still had a lot to offer.

But up in East Hull, beer cans were spraying at the news that Justin Morgan's Hull KR had just gone up. After years in the doldrums they had made the Super League.

Now there's a thing.

11

Nine Minute Miracle

1992 – 1995
Goroka

Believe it or not I learnt to drive in a police car. I know John McLane wouldn't believe it, neither would Steve MacNamara, or countless other people who've sat in a car with me. But it's true.

When I look back, I think that when the Goroka police formed a rugby team, that was one of the moments in my life that opened a lot of doors for me. Not just giving me the chance to drive, but also for the first time I knew where I was going.

And the doors didn't open just for me. Life in the settlement back then didn't offer a lot of chances for many people. Sure, Kaula had his shop there, and that helped us to buy what we couldn't get from the land. But for a lot of younger guys there was nothing to do, and no real way of making money. That's why the Rascals had been running for so long. Partly to steal stuff, but I also think the main reason was to just fill the day.

So when the police chief, Joe Bulhage, saw that kids were just hanging about on the streets smoking dope, he came up with the great idea to form the police team, the Royals. He got it together with a guy called John Supa, who's now a journalist back in PNG. And he did it at a very important time for me and my mates.

Most of the local rugby teams at the time were formed in the villages. A few of the bigger villages had their own teams. But in the settlement, people come and go, so there isn't the same strength of community there. And there was no one with enough power or influence to form a team.

When the Royals police team was brought together, as I said before, some of the Rascals thought that it was a trap. They really thought that they would turn up at the training ground, and all the police would jump out and shout 'Boo' and arrest them! But that just shows that there had never been any real contact or trust at all between them and the police. I'm not so naïve to think that police don't play dirty from time to time all over the world; over here in the UK they jump out of bushes onto the roads, waving a speed gun and shouting 'Boo', and scaring the shit out of anyone who drives past!

But Joe had a lot more class. And I, as well as a lot of my mates, saw this as a great chance to have a team, and play proper footy. He really had hit on a brilliant idea and it definitely changed my life. I have absolutely no doubt that if he hadn't formed the Royals, I would never have played for the Kumuls, never come to Hull, never met Jo, never eaten a doner kebab...I could go on for ever. God knows where I would have been.

When I look back at my life and all the chances I have had to see things I could never have dreamed up in my head, Joe Bulhage is the guy. All the time that I've been in the UK, it seems that whenever I've needed a hand up, something has happened, or someone has been there to help me. But it would all have been nothing if I hadn't started playing for the Royals in the first place.

I made the team in 1992, and I just loved playing my footy in a real team. It was nothing like the set ups that I've seen in the UK, but to me it was fantastic. We were getting good coaching and the police were giving us kits and boots to wear.

At the time the Goroka police had a very fierce mobile squad. They were kind of like reinforcement troops if there was trouble anywhere in the country. So quite often a group of them would go down to Port Moresby for a couple of weeks. Whenever there was a lot of fighting anywhere they'd go to help to sort it out; they'd do two weeks on and then come home for one week. They were almost like an army corps, going out for a short stint when fighting was at its worst, like the UK boys going out to Afghanistan.

But it was great for us, because when they went down to Port Moresby in particular, they would bring home the very best boots and equipment. I know how important that was for all of us, to give us the help to play the best footy we possibly could. And in turn that gave me a chance to make something of myself. So whenever I have been home, every single year of the last twelve, I have always gone to see the police boys; I always take them a case of beer. It's just a small repayment for everything they gave to me.

And the boys at Bradford won't be surprised to hear that there was one perk that I got that made up my mind that this was definitely the life for me. There were three or four of us that were playing good rugby every week and so the police looked after us really well. They told us to come to the single policemen's barracks to get our food. We had breakfast, lunch and dinner down there. As you can imagine this was like a dream come true for me. I could see why the single policemen were in no hurry to get married!

And, of course, it was at the police barracks that I took the first steps to becoming the outstanding driver that I am today! What actually happened was that the police were getting so excited that the Royals were doing well in the league, that they gave me the keys to a police car so that I could practice. It's amazing what doors do open when you can play footy a bit.

If only Crooksy could have seen me driving backwards and forwards in the compound. The police just left me to it, and so a week later when I asked for a driving licence they gave me one.

I'm sorry to all the people I nearly killed on Holderness Road four years later, but at the time it saved me an awful lot of hassle! That's a bit of an exaggeration because I think that driving tests back home aren't too difficult. And it's a lot easier driving over there, because you only see about ten or fifteen other cars a day. You just have to watch out for pigs and chickens.

♦

Life was just great. I was playing footy every weekend, and training through the week. And in a way, I was looking after myself for the first time, because I got all my meals with the police and had a lot of my kit paid for. So I was making my own contribution to the family in that way. I spent some of my time down at the settlement with Kaula and Maul, and some up at the village with Mum and Ben. Oh, and of course my little brother Martin was three by now. Ben, who was five years older, was getting bigger and stronger, and he liked to run around and play footy with me. So everything was sweet.

And I loved being involved with the Royals. I was getting looked after really well. They used to drive up to our village every Sunday morning to pick me up for the game. But they weren't particularly subtle. The first time they turned up it caused a bit of a scare in the village. It was a peaceful and sunny morning, and everybody was just going about their normal business when the marked police car drove in, with lights flashing and sirens blazing.

All the kids who were just hanging around smoking marijuana heard the car and then threw their spliffs into the bush and ran off. The older boys who were playing cards turned their tables over and hurried out of sight. And then the car drew up to Mum's, everybody looking from behind a tree or from inside their houses. I thought it was really funny as I jumped into the car with my kitbag and we just sped off.

Uncle Dixon, who was one of the boys playing poker, didn't:
"That wasn't really necessary for the police boys to drive in with the lights on and making that racket. It scared the shit out of us Stanley. And I had two bloody queens!"

Point taken. But I didn't say anything to the boys and the following week, exactly the same thing happened again. There were kids swallowing lit joints, chickens scattering, pigs charging and card tables crashing. I couldn't be bothered to ask the police not to do it, it just seemed like fun to me.

But everyone in the village was getting more and more pissed off, and during the week one of the village elders went to see the police to ask them not to make such a commotion every Sunday. He asked them to be a bit lower key when they came to pick me up, because they were upsetting the locals. The message was received and understood. So the weekend after everything returned to normal, the old boys could play cards, the young boys could get stoned and the pigs could have a shit in peace.

But I was getting really friendly with the police, and Joe Bulhage had become like an uncle to me. I felt like I could ask them for anything, within reason. There was one time when I needed a car because I was going to see some mates in another village. So I asked one of the police if I could borrow one. He took me round the back of the station and pointed to an old Toyota that had been impounded because it had no tax. As he gave me the keys he said:

"You can take that one, but only drive it around at night and bring it back on Monday morning!"

Fantastic, but it did cut down my options a bit. I did what I was told, and so that might explain one or two things that happened when I first arrived in Hull. In PNG I had only driven on roads where there were no other cars, and only in the dark. So you can understand why I was dazzled by the glare when I first got in my car at Craven Park!

♦

I played for the Royals from 1992 to 1994 in the Goroka league and we did well. In 1992 we won most of the matches that we played, and at the end of the season I had my first experience of a really big game. We reached the Grand Final for the league and we were playing at the Goroka Stadium. It was a great achievement for the Royals, because we'd only been formed the year before and out of the ten teams in the Goroka league we finished up in the top two.

The final was between the Royals and the Wardens. I thought it was weird that the prison wardens were playing against a police team that was half full of ex Rascals. It's funny how things turn out sometimes!

But it was a fantastic day. When I ran out for the Royals there were hundreds of supporters there cheering, and flares were going off. All my family was there and the Police Chief was in the stadium as well. I don't remember that much about the game after that, but I know that we won. And I had got a taste that would never go away for the next sixteen years.

I must have played okay in the final because at the beginning of the following season I was selected to play for Goroka. The best players in the Goroka league were picked to represent the city in the national league. To play for Goroka was like a dream come true, and it was a real honour.

It was about this time that Kaula and Uncle Dixon and my other uncles back in the village were getting right behind me. I had always known that I had a family that would do anything for me, but now I was giving them something to be proud of. I think I was the first player from our village and settlement to represent Goroka and I wasn't about to screw up the chance.

Goroka played in the Island League, and it was the nearest thing back home to Super League because there were eight clubs, and we travelled around playing teams like Lae and Moresby. And for the first time in my life I was getting paid for playing footy. Okay I had free food and boots from the Royals, but this was cold, hard cash in my hand. We got seventy five Kinas a game, which is about twenty quid.

Some of the older boys had other jobs as well, but I had only one aim now and I was completely focussed on my footy. Rugby was quickly starting to become my whole life. I still helped out back home in Kaula's shop and on Christina's land, but the rest of the time I was playing or training; either for the Royals or the Goroka city team.

Playing for Goroka really opened my eyes to how seriously guys back home take rugby league. Our training was better organised and much harder, and we went out every week with a burning need to win. And that passion spread to the terraces as well, where the supporters sometimes seemed to think the game was a matter of life and death. It was a pretty dangerous pastime watching footy, and sometimes playing it as well.

I remember a few games where the fans were pelting us with slingshots during the match. If we were playing away, all sorts of stuff would be flying down at us, rocks, pieces of wood and metal. You only realised what was happening when our winger started to creep in towards the middle. We'd be shouting, 'hey get back out there', and then we'd watch him get hit by a half brick!'

Sometimes it went way over the top. We had a real grudge thing with the team from Mendi, which was about fifty miles away. At one match when we played there, some guys tried to blow up our team bus with kerosene. And so the next time we played Mendi we had to play on a neutral ground half way between the two. The tension was incredible, and we could see that trouble was brewing. The fans were armed with bush knives and sling shots; I guess the security check on the way into the ground didn't quite happen! And as expected when we won the game it kicked off big style. But it wasn't just an after match pitch battle. The fight blew up for the next few weeks. The worst of it was in Goroka but anybody who was obviously on foreign ground was in danger.

The guys driving government vehicles were like sitting ducks, because their vans had a different mark on them depending on where they came from. Mendi vans had a bit of black paint on them and Goroka vans had a red mark. I often saw government vehicles getting pushed down a valley. And you thought that Hull KR fans didn't really like Hull F.C.!

It was pretty scary back home in those days, but things seem to have calmed down a bit over the last few years. It's more of a sport now, and some fans are even saying, 'win or lose – we'll try again next week.' But while things on the terraces were pretty tough, life on the pitch, when I could avoid getting hit by rocks was getting better all the time.

I was still having a great time playing for the police, but the Goroka team was doing better than anyone had expected, and at the end of the season we made the final of the inter-city South Pacific Cup. The final was at Port Moresby and we were playing against Moresby. It was kind of like Hull KR playing Saints in the Challenge Cup Final, apart from the fact that Moresby were at home.

We'd been playing better and better through the season, and no one from back home was surprised when we lifted the cup. We were the first team outside the capital ever to take the SP Cup home, and as you can imagine it sparked some great celebrations.

I was still a young kid, somewhere around twenty, I can't quite work it out, and I had the world at my feet. Well at the very least I had the country at my feet. All the kids and old boys in the village, and in Goroka, were getting more and more excited about the Rugby, and I was starting to get recognised when I walked down the street in the city.

◆

I always promised myself that if I ever had the chance, then I'd bring water to our village. All my life I had walked down to the creek to get water for washing and Kaula and his dad before him had done the same. When water was put into the town, God knows how long ago, they could have connected the last mile up to our village. But they didn't; the money that was there to do the work 'went somewhere else'.

I always thought it was shameful for little kids from our village to have to take a bucket whenever they went into town. They'd have to leave it in the bush and before coming back home fill it up wherever they could, or from the creek.

I'd done that right through school, and I was getting fed up with having to go to the creek just to have a wash. And if we waited for the government to connect the water we'd still be waiting now. The money had already been spent.

This had been the first year when I was earning real money for playing footy. And as it turned out, the team manager from Goroka was a bank manager, and one day he asked us all if we wanted to open a bank account with him. Two or three of us said 'yes' and I was pretty keen to get an account. So after the first week when I was paid, of the seventy five Kinas I always took twenty five Kinas home and put the other fifty in my bank account.

Then after we won the S P Cup in Port Moresby, we were all given five hundred Kinas. That was a bloody fortune – about a hundred quid!

And put together with the money I'd saved throughout the season, I had enough to buy the pipes and joints to cover the three quarters of a mile from the town to our village.

So I said to all the guys in the village, 'boys, we're getting up early tomorrow and we're going to start digging'.

And we did. From five o'clock in the morning to nightfall we dug the ditch. The day after, we laid the pipes down and we got these two guys who were plumbers from Goroka to connect it all up.

We put a tap in right at the front of the village. And it was one of the proudest moments of my life when we turned it, and out came some drops of water. I'd finally managed to do something for the village where I was born and my family and friends had got something that I hoped would improve their lives. And kids wouldn't have to go through the shame of carrying a bucket around town any more.

The water system wasn't perfect. A couple of the houses in the village were higher up and so if we turned our water on lower down, all the water pressure blasted the water out to us and the houses up there dried out! But it was a start.

♦

At the beginning of 1994 there was a military coup in PNG. Down in Bougainville the fighting started after the people there had got pissed off with the government exploiting them. Bougainville was where all the copper mines in the country were, and the government was using all the copper without making any payment.

So the Bougainville Revolutionary Army, the BRA (no kidding), started to fight to try to get independence and form its own country. We didn't really know what was happening down there until one day an old school mate of mine told me that his brother, who was in the army, had been killed down there.

And for the first time the impact of the coup had reached us up here in the mountains. We felt that we were affected now because one of our own boys had been killed. A lot of fighting broke out in Goroka, because anyone from Bougainville was getting attacked and beaten up. You could tell where they were from because they were very black, they had much darker skin than us.

The reprisals carried on all year and I guess as kids in the army came from all over the country there was trouble all over the place. Our city was affected for quite a while and there was a bad feeling on the streets. It made me realise how fierce the loyalty of people in PNG is, and how they look after their own. But by the middle of the year, the BRA had been taken apart and things got back to normal. In the end I don't think we would have even noticed if my mate's brother hadn't been killed.

◆

On the footy field that year I had another good season and at the end of the year I got a call that I just couldn't believe. The chairman of selectors for the PNG national team had been on the phone to my coach at Goroka; and I found out that I'd been selected to play for the Colts team against France.

Ben went crazy when I told him, and I was finding it hard to get my head around it. I'd only been playing for the Royals for two years, but now I was going to play for PNG. On every tour the selectors always pick the Kumuls team and a Colts team, so I had the chance to see some of the best players in the country and maybe find out just how good I actually was.

There were three guys I knew from the Goroka team who were picked for the Kumuls at the same time so there was a lot of pride in the city. I couldn't wait to pull on the PNG shirt and I didn't have to wait for long, because the first Colts game was the weekend after the end of the season.

I remember thinking, as I flew down to Madang to meet up with the rest of the team, that everything had gone right for me from the moment I started playing for the police. In our first season, the Royals had won the Goroka League Final, and in my first year playing for Goroka we won the SP Cup in Port Moresby. And now I was on my way to play for my country!

On the afternoon of the game the stadium in Madang was absolutely packed. It wasn't a very big ground and it held about 6,000 fans, but there were thousands outside the ground when we arrived. And it was a blistering hot day. My whole memory of the game is a little bit cloudy, but I do remember that from the moment we ran out onto the field the French boys were complaining. I don't think they were too happy with the changing facilities, but the main thing was that they just couldn't stand the heat.

We were getting pretty fed up that the game was all stopping and starting and I thought the French were just trying to hold up our play. But when I came over to England two years later I realised that they were actually suffering quite a lot. As you know, in my first season at Hull I ran off the field during a game to get warm, so I then understood what their problem had been.

But the crowd didn't, and they were getting really pissed off when the game kept stopping every ten minutes or so; they were used to seeing non-stop action. So I don't know if it was a cheer of joy or relief when the final whistle went. It was joy for me and the boys because we'd won as the French wilted in the sun. But it was definitely relief for the French boys as they trooped off, some of them could hardly walk. And to make matters worse I think they had forgotten that the showers were a mile away!

♦

It was a great night. After the game, we went to the hotel and got showered, and I was stopping over in Madang until my flight the next morning; so that gave me the chance to hang around the pool and have a few beers. Even though there were a couple of guys from Mendi there, we were really happy and having a great time celebrating. Three of the Colts team were playing for the Kumuls the next day in Port Moresby, so they were getting ready to head off to the airport. And I was just cracking open my second beer when the chairman of the selectors called me over:

"Stanley mate, you're going to be flying to Port Moresby tonight."

"Why?"

All I could think was that there was a spare seat on the plane and they wanted me to go on to help out and get some experience. Not quite, as it turned out:

"You're going to be playing Stanley, so put the beer down."

Had I heard him right? Well he definitely said 'put the beer down' so if he was kidding it was a very shit joke. But he certainly wasn't drunk. And he told me that Mark Mom, one of the colts that were going to play for the Kumuls the next day, had twisted his ankle. There was no chance of him recovering in time for the first test and so I had got the call. This was the most incredible thing that had ever happened to me, well certainly in the game. And my head was all over the place, it was like a fantastic dream. But it was true.

I was on the flight within an hour, and only two hours after I'd 'put the beer down' I was in the hotel with the Kumuls. They hadn't expected to see me there and even though I knew a few of them it was still an awesome moment for me. The best players in the country were there, it was the night before a test match with France and I was there too. I just told them that I was there to watch the game, I don't really know why. Maybe I thought they wouldn't believe me because I was still trying to believe it myself.

When we sat down for dinner the chairman stood up at the end of the table and said:

"Okay guys, can you all welcome Stanley, he's taking Mark Mom's place."

And straight away the boys were saying 'well done mate' and shaking my hand, and for the first time I felt like I belonged there, with the PNG Kumuls ... bloody hell.

I slept like a tree that night and when I woke up I stared at the ceiling, and suddenly realised where I was and what I was doing there. It's that kind of feeling that I had every morning when I first arrived in the UK. In some ways it didn't seem real, and when I opened my eyes and saw what was around me I just thanked God. I still get that feeling sometimes, and it makes me feel very lucky.

But then I realised that Mum and everyone in the village were expecting me home that morning. I wouldn't have been surprised if they'd already killed a pig! So I jumped out of bed and got on the phone to Mum. I kind of thought from the tone of Mum's voice that she was wondering what I was up to. But I know now that she was shocked by what I had told her and was also very, very proud. And Maul told me some time later that when Kaula found out that I was going to be playing for the Kumuls he broke the biggest smile she had ever seen in her life. Then he went to have a beer with some of his old mates and when he came back in the afternoon he was still smiling from ear to ear. And that meant more to me than anything.

I just wished that Kaula could have been there to see me when I walked out with the team at the Lloyd Robson Oval. I was looking around me in amazement. The ground was packed to the rafters, and there were trucks all around the outside with guys crammed onto each roof. All the trees were taken by the branch managers, there seemed to be ten or fifteen guys on each tree. And when we walked out the whole place went completely crazy.

And this was the day when I had what I call my 'nine minute miracle'. It was a day I'll never forget, which I guess it should be. My first full international playing for the PNG Kumuls, I was bursting with pride, and I took my seat on the bench, grabbed a bottle of water and started to focus.

The first half seemed to go in a flash. It was a tight game with not a lot of chances, and again I think the stifling heat was getting to the French side so there were a lot of breaks. When I took my seat for the second half I was sure that I'd get on, it was just a matter of time. But the seconds went by, and the minutes, and soon we were half way through the second half. And it wasn't all going to plan on the pitch. It was always going to be a tough game against France, and they seemed to be grinding us down. With about ten minutes left we were 22-14 down and I just thought it wasn't going to be my day, or the team's for that matter.

Then I got the call to get on. This was it, the biggest moment of my playing career. I had less than ten minutes to play so I just wanted to make the best impression I could. And I had a dream start. I was getting into the action really quickly and seeing a lot of the ball. With about five minutes left on the clock I made a break, took a big hit and managed to squeeze the ball out to David Buko who went over for a try.

What a start. I couldn't believe my luck. The boys were all hugging me and slapping me on the back and the adrenalin was gushing through me.

I just wanted to stay focussed, make sure I didn't cock anything up and drive for all I was worth. I had to give everything I had for myself and the team. And two minutes later I got the chance to break again and this time I went over myself. The whole stadium erupted and at least three branch managers dropped out of their trees. We'd come from behind to lead with only a couple of minutes left. I was in dreamland.

I was sure we were going to hold on, when I kicked a goal and the place went completely mental again. The noise hadn't died down when the final hooter went and the fans rushed onto the pitch. We had beaten France 26-22 and I had set up a try, scored one and kicked a goal. If that wasn't a nine minute miracle then I'm a vegetarian! And those nine minutes changed my life forever.

♦

I was now a PNG Kumul. And after the France test I kept my place for the New Zealand tour in the same year. That was an experience, I can tell you! If I'm honest I think we never really had a chance to beat New Zealand. They were so much bigger than us and this was the first time that I had come across some of the very best players in the world. Reuben Wiki was playing. He's now an absolute god in Australia, and the team was littered with big stars. It was the first time I came up against Henry Paul. We were both playing number six at the time and it was a fantastic benchmark for me to work to if I wanted to become a great player.

Even though we struggled to compete on even terms with New Zealand the whole squad was pumped up that year, and everyone was busting a gut to play to their very best. There's a lot of pride in the Kumuls back home and each player who's lucky enough to pull on the shirt knows that. But there was more excitement than usual because 1995 was the World Cup to be held in England, and everyone wanted to be there. It seemed crazy to me that I now was in a position to have a chance of making the squad. But I wanted it more than anything I had ever wanted in my whole life.

I remember that the twenty five man squad was going to be announced on the radio, but up in the mountains we couldn't get a good reception. So I sent Ben down to Goroka to get a local newspaper. He was about eleven now, so he could run down and back in ten minutes or so. But for those ten minutes I just paced up and down. I didn't know what to do with myself and I wished that I had gone to get the paper rather than sending Ben.

So I sat on the steps outside Mum's house to wait. And then I could see Ben coming up the road holding a newspaper. He wasn't shouting anything at me so I thought maybe I hadn't made it. But then as he approached the house I could see a big smile on his face and I knew that I was in the squad.

I felt kind of numb. So much had happened to me over the past twelve months but this was the biggest thing ever. I was going to go to the other side of the world to England to play in the World Cup. Jesus, I just couldn't believe it. But the headlines were there with my face splashed all over the paper ….incredible. There were pictures of the four Goroka boys who had made the team, David Buko, Tuiyo Eviai David Gomia and me.

And now I had a new found celebrity status. As I've said, rugby league is like a religion back home, and for the next few days I was getting bought beers by people I didn't know, and I couldn't walk down the street without someone shouting out my name.

But I didn't have much time to celebrate. We had to get tickets to fly down to Port Moresby to join up with the rest of the squad. We had a week's training down at the capital before we set off to play our warm up games; and the World Cup was only three weeks away.

So I said goodbye to Mum and Ben, Maul and Kaula and I was off to Europe. I'd done plenty of flying before in Papua New Guinea. Travelling by road in the mountain regions is so difficult that there are little airstrips all over the place, and going by plane to me was like travelling by train is to you. But I'd never been so far before. I'd just flown a few hundred miles here and there but now I was on my way to the other side of the world.

◆

We flew straight to France for our warm up games. There was no language difficulty for me in going to France first, because I couldn't speak English either! To me, it seemed just like we were going to a country that was part of England, like the South Sea Islands are all linked together. But having been there a few times since, I now know that there are big differences between the two countries.

And one of the biggest problems is the food. I couldn't stand it. We were eating that bun all the time, what do you call it – a baguette. We were eating it for breakfast when we got up, and in the evening when we went to bed. And for bloody lunch as well. I was just dying to have some rice and chicken or chips or something.

It didn't affect our warm up too much, we just had two games, won one and lost one and then we headed off to England. Now that I've been to France a lot I know how to get good food. I usually go out for a pizza; there are pizza restaurants and vans everywhere. Someone told me that the pizza was actually invented in France so why the hell do they eat so many baguettes?

The second thing I've learnt is that you must always drink wine with your meal – and that does make it a lot better. But you drink it by the glass and not the bottle; I've struggled with that sometimes. And the seafood is fantastic. But we didn't know all this at the time and so stuffed with bread we gladly flew off to the food capital of Europe, North Ferriby, which is in Hull.

We were all staying at this big hotel called the Forte Post house in North Ferriby. And when we found the restaurant we discovered that our prayers had been answered. The menu read' 'Fish and Chips; Chicken and Chips; Steak and Kidney Pudding…' I had no idea what the third one was but who cared? All we had to do was to get them to cook the fish and the chickens. But this was easier said than done because we couldn't speak English properly. We had two tour managers, James Korona, and Jim Robinson, who was Australian – so we would have to rely a lot on Jim.

And Adrian Lam had travelled around the world before so he took charge; he knew how to do things over here. He explained that when they take your order, they go and cook everybody's and then bring them all out at the same time. That seemed like a pretty stupid idea because there were thirty of us. It must be impossible. Anyway Adrian seemed to know what he was doing so he shouted out, 'Who wants fish and chips?' and so on. About six or seven of us put our hands up for fish and chips and then we sat down to wait. And wait….

In the meantime someone came out and said they'd run out of chickens so could two guys have fish instead? I kind of thought, 'how can a restaurant run out of chickens – is there no school nearby?' but two of the boys put their hands up and we carried on waiting. Then Adrian looked out of the window and said:

"Hey look, they've run out of fish as well."

And he pointed out of the window at two little boats that were floating on the River Humber. We couldn't believe it. We were going to be here for ages. By the time they'd caught however many fish they needed, rowed back and cooked them, it'd be midnight. I was gutted. We were all whinging and some of us went up to James and said, 'just give us some money and we'll go and get a takeaway.' We'd seen some KFC's and MacDonald's on the way so that would have to do.

And then the doors to the kitchen swung open and out came nine fish and twenty chickens! How the hell did they manage to do that? That was a real 'nine minute miracle'. I sat down to eat my fish and chips and looked round to see that the two boats were still there. God knows how they did it!

♦

We had a couple of days for sightseeing before our first match which was against Tonga at the Boulevard in Hull. We all went around the city taking photos and buying stuff. And I even got a picture of myself in the car park outside Craven Park. I wanted to get photos of the places that I would probably never get to visit again.

I thought it must have been the cold season in England. It was the beginning of October and it was bloody freezing. But we noticed that when they went out at night, the boys just wore t – shirts and the girls had really short skirts. They looked very funny but they seemed to be having a good time.

As we walked out of the tunnel and onto the pitch at the Boulevard, I had forgotten about the cold and I was trying to stay right in my zone. This was the biggest game of my short career by a million miles, and I was walking out with some of the best players in the world. Adrian Lam was my idol, and I was so proud to be walking out onto the pitch with him. I was number six and he was seven – I couldn't have picked a better guy to be alongside.

It was a game that a lot of people remember because we went in at half time 22-0 down. Tonga was a strong side and they had run us ragged in the first half. But we came out in the second half and played a blinder and we ended up drawing the game 28-28. I felt like I'd played really well, so the fish and chips tasted pretty good that night.

I got up early the next morning; I think my head was still buzzing so I went down to the restaurant to have breakfast before the training for the day started. While I was eating my cereal one of the boys came over to me and said that this white guy had been looking for me. It turned out to be Colin Hutton who was on the board of Hull Kingston Rovers and he was still in the hotel. I couldn't speak much English at all, so I asked Jim Robinson if he'd talk to this bloke for me.

Ten minutes later Jim came back and told me that Mr Hutton wanted to speak to me and our number four, John Okul. He was interested in both of us and wanted to talk about a move to play over here in England, and he'd left his phone number. But I was a bit scared to speak to him so I just left my address and thought no more about it.

The whole World Cup was a fantastic experience for me. I loved every minute of it and it had really opened my eyes. We didn't play that much footy though because we had to beat New Zealand at St Helens to make it through to the quarter finals. And from the very first minute when Kevin Iro ran half the length of the field in what seemed like a second, they absolutely ran riot.

But I'd been given the chance to play on the world stage only three years after I'd started playing for the police team in Goroka. And I didn't know it at the time, but soon enough another big door was going to swing wide open right in front of me.

◆

I've had a lot of good times over the years playing for the Kumuls and seen a lot of great places. I always love going on tour because every where's different and so I would never say that I had any bad tours. Sure we were beaten sometimes and sometimes quite badly. Going to Australia or New Zealand was never easy and we weren't always as competitive as we wanted to be. Quite often by the time a tour came round we were all knackered because we'd played so much rugby, wherever we were in the world. But a tour's a tour and every single day is exciting. And we've had some great players over the years, but none were better than Adrian Lam. He was so quick and has a brilliant mind for footy. It's obvious that he's now made the step up to becoming our national coach really well.

I liked going to Samoa, and Fiji was brilliant too. It's a fantastic country, the people are great and we always have good games there. I always think that Internationals are brilliant to play in but the best times were always in the World Cup.

My second World Cup came around in 2000. It was in England and France again and it would have been a year earlier but it clashed with the Rugby Union World Cup. By that time of course I was living in England, up in Hull, so I knew all about the customs and how to get along. This time I was able to help some of the younger guys.

Before the Kumuls squad came over to Europe I rang one of my uncles back home to see if there were any Goroka boys in the team. My uncle said, 'yeah, there's only one, it's this kid called Makali Aizue.' I thought to myself, 'that surname rings a bell' and then it came to me. I knew his family pretty well. I knew his mum and dad and sister, and I knew all his four brothers, but for some reason I'd never met him until he joined the 2000 World Cup squad. He was originally from Madang, but he'd been brought up in Goroka. And like me he played for the police team and the Goroka team before he made the Kumuls.

I soon found out that Makali's a great kid, and I spoke to him a lot during the two weeks we were at the World Cup. At the end, before he went home I told him to keep working hard at his game and I knew he'd do well. I kept hearing how he was doing back home and a year or so later I rang Neil Hudgell to tell him about Makali. So Neil brought him over and he's now the longest serving player at Craven Park.

♦

At the start of the 2000 World Cup I thought that we had a good chance to make it through to the quarter-finals at least. We weren't in an easy group, but we had a fair chance in each of the games. We were in with France, South Africa and Tonga, with all the matches being played in France. All the bookies had Tonga as the clear favourites to go through, but our confidence started to grow right away when we beat France in Paris.

And we were starting to attract some attention when we beat Tonga. That was a tough game and I remember Willy Mason, the Australian prop was playing for Tonga at the time. But Adrian Lam was on fire, and I'm pretty sure that Wigan decided to sign him when they saw him at his best in this tournament. And I wouldn't be at all surprised if it had something to do with my move to Gateshead the season after as well.

All we had to do was beat South Africa to go through and sure enough, at the end of the week we were on our way to England. We'd won all three of our games and we'd made it to the quarters - fantastic. I couldn't wait to get over there and show the guys around, and we definitely felt that we had the momentum now and we could go a long way.

For some reason we were staying at a hotel way up in Northumberland. After we got a flight over to the UK we started the long coach trip up to the hotel. But we travelled at night and it was raining so we couldn't see where we were going but it was certainly a long way. We were all knackered but we were still buzzing, particularly as we'd beaten Tonga.

Eventually we made it up to the front of the Hotel. And as we were getting our bags off, James said, 'hey look guys, they've got a Tongan flag up there.' Either the hotel was owned by someone from Tonga, or more likely, they'd bought flags for all the teams that were in our group to cover all possibilities. They must have forgotten to take this Tongan flag down. So we wandered in to the hotel lobby expecting to see some PNG Kumuls flags inside. But not only were there posters of Tonga and Tongan flags everywhere, there was a massive banner hung over the reception saying:

"WELCOME TO THE TONGA RUGBY LEAGUE TEAM!"

The smile on the face of the receptionist who was wearing an 'I love Tonga' badge slowly disappeared as James handed over his passport. Then she looked around at all of us very carefully, and then at a twelve foot poster of the Tonga team.

The only way it could possibly have been better was if the manager had run in playing the Tongan national anthem on a trumpet and wearing a 'PNG is Shit' t-shirt. But there was no sign of Basil Fawlty anywhere so we just went to bed.

The quarter final was at Widnes, which made our stay in the Tonga theme hotel in Northumberland seem even more ridiculous. We were going to play Wales, and I wondered if they'd be surprised to see us as well. The way they played, I don't think they were surprised at all; in fact they seemed to be very well prepared. And guess who was playing prop for them. It was none other than Hull KR's current (Australian) coach Justin Morgan. I think he got to play for Wales on account of his name.

But I swear that when Morgs saw me and Makali in front of him he shit in his pants! He denies it now and he just reminds us how the game went. We made a bright start and it was very close in the first ten minutes. But then Adrian threw a long pass that was intercepted by Iestyn Harris and he scored. For the next seventy minutes they smashed us to pieces and we were on our way home.

♦

There's always something very special about pulling on the Kumuls shirt and running out to play for your country. And I think that when I first got the call back in 1994 that made it clear to me that this was going to be my life, wherever I found myself in the world. And as I said before, the 1995 World Cup eventually opened another door for me which I went through and never looked back.

When Colin Hutton had tried to speak to me in the Post House in Hull, I didn't have the confidence to speak to him. I couldn't have understood him anyway so when I just left my address I went home thinking no more about it. But I was starting to wonder what the next step for me would be. I knew of some guys who wanted to play the game full time professionally had gone to Samoa or Australia. But I never dreamed of going back over to England.

That was until one morning when a package arrived in the post for me. It was a long letter that I couldn't read, a load of footy programmes from Hull KR and a video. Of course we didn't have electricity in the village but the video cover was nice. And when I spoke to Kaula and my uncles about it, they both said that I should go. It was a chance for me to see the world. And the club had sent me a two way ticket so I could come back home straight away if I wanted to.

Probably the thing that made up my mind was when they told me that my mate John Okul was coming over with me. Which made me think that I should go and try my luck. And so that was it, I was on my way to a new country to live and play, to a land where there was a KFC on every corner, and really white girls wear shorts when it snows, it was a cultural wonderland. And everybody at home was happy for me. Everybody that is, except Christina.

It wasn't that she wasn't proud of me; I think she just had a mother's instinct that it wasn't the right thing for me to do. I know that she was still holding out hope that I would go on one day to become a teacher. And she had worked so hard to pay for me to go right through school. But she could see in my eyes that it was something that I wanted to do. Rugby was my life and it was the best chance I had of making something of myself. So eventually I went with Mum's blessing, after I promised I'd ring home every day and eat lots of greens.

I had a lot of people to say goodbye to, friends, family and all the guys I'd played rugby with. I invited the police, the Goroka players and all the guys from the village team. And we had a big feast, after all, at this time I didn't know all about Chinese food so I couldn't be sure what my next meal would be. We had a massive roast with a sheep and Kaula cooked a goat as well.

Oh, and of course we killed a pig.

12

Red, Red Wine

2008
Hull Kingston Rovers

Wake me up someone. I must have been dreaming. The last thing that I remembered was that we'd just beaten Hull 42-6 at the K.C. Stadium to stay in the Super League. And I'd scored a try that had helped to make us safe. But it just didn't seem real in any way. I couldn't see properly and I wasn't at all sure where I was. Then slowly my eyes focussed on a clock at the side of the bed and I knew immediately where I'd found myself. So I started to lift my body....

SHIT! I felt like I'd been smashed over the head by a pig with a baseball bat, who had then crapped in my mouth. Actually, of course, there was no superhuman pig on a revenge mission; I must have drunk a few beers last night:

"Morning Stan, how're you feeling honey?"

Normally the sight of Jo opening the curtains and bringing me a cup of tea is one of those things that really make me happy. But I have to say, the sudden glare of blinding light just made things worse at this point in time.

But the one consolation to my miserable condition was that I hadn't been dreaming at all. We had just stuffed Hull in their own backyard and we were in the Super League again next year. What a fantastic day it had been, and a spectacular night by all accounts. I tried to smile, didn't quite make it and fell back to sleep.

The state I was in, by the time I'd made a full recovery the new season would have started! But over the next few weeks a lot happened at the club and there was so much to look forward to. In the close season Justin was hard at work and recruitment at the club was stronger than ever. A lot of top quality players like Ben Galea, Clint Newton, Garrett Crossman and Chev Walker, Daniel Fitzhenry and Jake Webster had made their way to Craven Park and activity at the club was starting to raise a few eyebrows. I think there's no single reason why players of this class are coming here. It's a combination of the coach, the board, and the fans play a massive part. The club's been really well marketed and now it looks like a top Super League team. I keep reading in the papers how well run the club is now.

And so far it's carried on through the season. We've just signed Michael Dobson. I know that Hull were tracking him for the last couple of months but as soon as we came in for him he signed without hesitation. That just shows how far we've come and how we can now compare ourselves with our fiercest rivals.

The first match of this season was my testimonial game against Castleford. I never even dreamed that I'd get a testimonial, I had another year on my contract with Rovers and I was looking forward to the new season more than ever. To me I always thought the word 'testimonial' was always linked to 'retirement', and nothing was further from my mind.

But I was grateful that the club showed me so much strong feeling to grant a testimonial. It made me realise now that this was always a two-way love affair. And when I walked onto the pitch it was a very emotional moment for me. Jo was there, and I walked on with Elliott and Leo. And when I looked up and saw all the supporters standing up and clapping it gave me a shiver. I just thought back to 1996 when I first came here, not long over twenty years old. Back then I never thought about tomorrow, I just lived life to the full every single day. And now I was walking on with my two boys, an eleven year old and a one year old, in front of a full stadium. It gave me goose bumps again. And when they played 'Cheer up Stanley Gene' that made my day. I know that the 'Magnificent Two Hundred' will have been there, but these days they're always joined by thousands of others who will give everything they have for the team.

♦

The first league match was away at Leeds. We'd been chosen to play in the curtain raiser for the Super League against the champions, live on Sky on the Saturday evening. I don't think many people gave us a prayer but we did give them a fright and we only lost it quite late in the game. It gave us a lot of encouragement that we could live with the best this year and challenge for a top six place. And our belief was proved right when we beat Saints in our first home match.

Then it was off to France to play Catalans. I always look forward to this trip now as I've found out where the best pizzas are, and it's bound to be warmer than Hull. But I was kind of worried they'd cancelled my visa after a little fracas I caused in the airport the year before.

It was a really warm evening and all the boys had gone out for a beer after the game. We weren't flying back until the morning so we had all night in France. As I've said before, I'm amazed how much you English lads can drink, so by about ten I was done in and I made my way back to the hotel. But when I arrived there I got a bit of a second wind and I fancied another drink. I couldn't see anyone at the bar, but then, as luck would have it, I remembered that one of our sponsors had dropped a couple of cases of wine off for us, and they were in the lounge area. I knew that Neil quite fancied some of the wine; it was apparently good stuff so I decided I'd only open one bottle.

I couldn't find a bottle opener, so I smashed the top off a bottle of Chateau Something and had a taste. And it was good, 'a robust wine with a hint of blackberry and a pleasing finish' or as I saw it, 'full of alcohol'. Ten minutes later I convinced myself that they wouldn't miss two, so I bit the top off another bottle.

The story goes, and in all honesty I can't confirm either way, that when the boys came back a couple of hours later they found me lying on the restaurant floor, with my mouth covered in blood and surrounded by seven or eight broken and half empty bottles. And of course, I always say to anyone who claims to have seen me at the airport shouting at an Air France poster, and then falling over the baggage carousel ….. it was Makali!

But luckily this year I sailed through customs quicker than a yank could shout 'put your hands where I can see them boy!' And the game turned out to be a very special one for me. It was the day that I scored my 100th try for Rovers and that was a massive thing. It was a great two-pointer as well, because we were four points behind very late in the game.

Justin had brought me off for a breather and then with less than five minutes left he threw me on again. We were driving hard and with a minute to go I picked the ball up off a dummy about ten yards out on the last tackle. So I tried to kick it through for Ben, but it ricocheted off someone. Of course, because I'm so young I was the quickest to it! And when Cooky planted the two points we were home and dry.

♦

Justin's changed a lot this year. Last year he was pretty mad sometimes, but he got the job done. He's a young kid and you learn as you go, we all do. Last season was one of the hardest in his career, and he did really well to keep us up. But in a lot of ways there's even more pressure this year, because we've invested a lot of money in players and we're aiming for a top six finish.

Justin's becoming a great coach, and he'll get to the very top of the game, hopefully with Rovers. He's technically brilliant and he knows how to motivate the boys. And so when we came to the first derby game of this year we were all pumped up. After beating them in their own back yard last year we just couldn't wait to play them again. When I remember all the jokes about 'eight points for Hull' when we first came up, it made it all the sweeter when we took four off them. And the way we did it was brilliant.

We were determined to get the first two points off them this year, and we went into the game seeing no other result. We'd had a couple of slip ups, games that we should have won, but Hull was down in the bottom two and had no confidence. But I remember the game mostly for the weather. It was nice and sunny in the morning but by the time we kicked off there was a gale force ten sweeping sleet across the ground. It must have been the worst conditions I've ever played in.

We didn't get far enough ahead in the first half with the wind, and I think we went in with just a six point lead. And when we came out in the second half the weather had got worse. When Cooky took a conversion me and Fitzy were hanging on to each other to keep warm, and when Cooky kicked it he watched the ball end up behind him! Hull scored twice to make it 10-10 and we were under siege for the last ten minutes. We could hardly see but we were fighting for our lives. And when Danny Tickle hit the post twice, the poor lad, we thought we might hang on.

Then with two minutes to go, James Webster did the impossible. In the face of a terrible storm he somehow chipped over a drop goal to see us home 11-10. OH YEEES! The stadium erupted and we knew we'd beaten them again. It was a messy win, but in some ways I think it couldn't have been better for our fans. To watch us snatch a win like that and then see the few hundred Hull fans getting pissed wet through, and not being able to see the other end of the pitch where we scored, was just too good for some of our supporters! They'd suffered for so long and now it was their turn in the sun – so to speak.

And before they'd all stopped laughing we had the chance to do it again. This time we were at the Millennium Stadium, and as we'd done a few times this season, we got in a good position and failed to finish the game off. We made too many mistakes being sloppy and dropping the ball. So Hull came back at us and with five minutes to go we were behind again. I'd just been taken off so now I saw it just as our fans did, and it looked like we were going to blow it. But then Jake Webster took a pass from Ben Galea and he fought his way over the line. We were all jumping up and down on the bench and shouting with the fans. This was big. We'd done it again, and it reminded me just how far we'd come so quickly to take four points off Hull in the first half of the season.

Now it would be really stupid to say we'll get eight this year wouldn't it?

◆

This year's been my worst ever for bans. I've never been down to Leeds for disciplinary so much. The one that really pissed me off was the week before the Huddersfield game. I'd got a one match ban for a high tackle, which takes some doing when you're five foot six! Anyway, it meant that I was going to miss the home match with Huddersfield which was a real bummer. I was gutted because I hate missing games against teams that I've played for. And after Rovers, Huddersfield has to be the team that's most special to me in the UK.

I watched the first half from inside, but then I decided to come outside for the second half. I was looking around me to see where to sit when I saw Neil and Jo Hudgell. They were waving at me to go and sit with them so I made my way over.

As I was wandering across I heard a voice behind me:

"Hey Stan, what the hell are you doing up here?"

I looked up and it was Jon Sharp and three of his coaching team, and they were all wearing dark glasses and ear pieces. They looked like 'Reservoir Dogs' sat there, and I took my seat right in front of them. Then I got my mobile out and turned round to Jon and joked:

"Hey Jon, I'll listen to you, and then I'll ring Justin and tell him what you said."

Two minutes later when I turned round again all four of them had gone!

They must have done their job right because the Giants nicked a point. Hopefully that won't be one of those things that comes and bites us in the arse at the end of the year. There's plenty of time left and loads of points will be won and lost yet.

As you know I've spent plenty of time on the physio's couch over the past twelve years. And this season I've already had a couple of bits of treatment. I always seem to be able to get over injuries quickly thank God. I think it must be because I'm so young that I heal quickly. But whenever I've had treatment I always do what I'm told and do it right; I follow all the instructions from the physio or the doctor to the letter, and Jo makes sure that I do that as well. I just want to get back playing as soon as possible. One day injured is one too many for me, and I'll do everything I can to get back on the pitch.

Straight after our cup win against Huddersfield a couple of weeks ago, I had some keyhole surgery on my knee, to get rid of a bit of stuff that was floating around. The specialist said that I should be fit to play again in three to four weeks or so. But eleven days later I was on the field for our home game against Harlequins.

I was pleased to be back so soon and it was a good game to be involved in. It was Michael Dobson's home debut and he scored a couple of tries as we got a pretty good win. That took us to sixth place and we're now in a position to kick on. I got a try as well just to prove that I can even do it with only one leg!

We should finish in the top six. We've got the quality and the spirit to get there, with a great coach, a very supportive board, and the best fans in the country. It's just down to us now. Our problem is that we sometimes lose the really winnable games. Only last week we were stuffed by Huddersfield, but we've already shown that we can beat teams like Saints and Bradford. We all know what we need to do.

♦

So what comes next for Stanley Gene? Well if you'd told me what was going to happen to me twenty years ago, I would never have believed you. Back then if someone had said that I'd be able to play for Goroka that would have been fantastic on its own.

And I feel like I've settled into the way of life here in England over the past twelve years. It's been pretty difficult at times but I've had loads of laughs and made some great friends along the way. So me and Jo have no plans to move anywhere else, and why would we?

I want to carry on playing rugby for as long as I can. I know that you're thinking 'of course Stan's much too young to retire' but believe me it will come to us all one day. But as long as I can keep showing what I'm worth to the team I want to keep on playing. And I want to finish my career at Rovers. If I go on next year I don't want to be anywhere else.

This was the club that gave me a chance all those years ago, and it's difficult to explain in words just what Hull KR means to me. It's not just wearing the shirt and winning games, it's much more than that. Rovers is like another family. Neil said to me 'I'm not going to retire you Stan, that's something you'll decide when you're ready'. And when that day comes I'd love to stay in the game in some way. If I hadn't been a rugby player then I'd have wanted to be a teacher or a fireman, but footy has become my life.

And I have two other wonderful families. I know I've said this already but Jo's been my rock for the last eleven years. She's helped me through God knows what, and always kept me on the straight and narrow. We've had a lot of fun, but there've been some hard times too. I just want to be the best husband and dad that I possibly can.

And of course I have the best of both worlds. When my bollocks reach freezing point, I can always go back home to Goroka to see my folks. I'll always have family there. Christina's still young and Ben and Martin have now grown into men. And however long Maul is with me I'll want to be nearby. I hope Kaula's smiling down on me – if there are any other boys up there with him, he'll be boring the pants off them with stories about me playing footy. I know that he was proud of me and that means more than almost anything in the world.

Some things are still the same back home. There are still some pretty hairy spiders, and plenty of shitty snakes. Some of the guys in politics are still dodgy, but if they weren't I guess we'd be worried. Donald's still deaf in one ear. You can still eat tree worms and the greens and bananas are as great as they always were.

And while it's still a religion over there, more guys are seeing rugby as a game and not a war. And the game has a massive part to play in giving good messages out.

It's the world cup in Australia this year and I'll be there, hopefully breaking my balls for the mighty Kumuls again. We've got a good team now. A lot of the kids play for feeder clubs in New Zealand and Australia and they're getting better all the time. Look out for a young winger called Michael Mark; he's a brilliant prospect with a big future. I'd just love to play against England over there.

But I'll call home on the way to see all my family. Oh and we put electricity into the village last year, it's wired into my house and connected up to about six other houses in the village. So if I can find it, I'll watch the video that Rovers sent over to me in 1995 and decide whether I would have come! I don't think it would have made a difference.

I've been so lucky and I thank God that I've had two amazing lives to live. Jo has been over to PNG to see my world over there. And now it will mean more than anything to me if I can bring Maul and Christina to see my world over here.

I'm glad that you've seen a little bit of both.

Thank you.

Stan

Stanley Gene UK Career Statistics
(To 1st June 2008)

Season	Apps	Sub	Tries	Goals	Drop Goals	Points
			Hull Kingston Rovers			
1996	22	1	26	1	1	107
1997	32	1	23		1	93
1998	36		34		1	137
1999	18	1	11			44
2007	17	3	5			20
2008	14	5	2			8
Total	**139**	**11**	**101**	**1**	**3**	**409**
			Hull F. C.			
2000	7	15	8			32
2001	1	12	2			8
Total	**8**	**27**	**10**			**40**
			Huddersfield Giants			
2002	25	2	28			112
2003	21	1	9			36
2004	23	2	5			20
2005	19	2	7			28
Total	**88**	**7**	**49**			**196**
			Bradford Bulls			
2006	5	19	10			40
Total	**5**	**19**	**10**			**40**

Stanley has represented his country many times with distinction, and on a number of occasions as captain. Records held since his debut in 1994 are incomplete. Suffice to say Stanley has legendary status in Papua New Guinea and we suspect his international career is not yet over.